GW01090363

THE GAIA DIALOGUES

OTHER BOOKS BY MURRY HOPE

The Way of Cartouche
Practical Greek Magic
The Greek Tradition
Practical Celtic Magic
Practical Egyptian Magic
Practical Atlantean Magic
The Lion People
The Paschats and the Crystal People
The Psychology of Ritual
The Psychology of Healing
Practical Techniques of Psychic Self-Defence
The 9 Lives of Tyo
The Book of Talimantras
Ancient Egypt: The Sirius Connection
Atlantis: Myth or Reality?
Essential Woman: Her Mystery, Her Power
Olympus: An Experience of Self-Discovery
Time: The Ultimate Energy

All Murry Hope's books are available from Thoth Publications. If you live in the U.K., and wish to receive a catalogue, send two first class stamps and a self-addressed envelope to: Thoth Publications, 98 Ashby Road, Loughborough, Leicestershire, LE11 3AF, England. Tel: 01509 210626.

Those who reside outside the U.K. please enclose U.S. $2.00 to offset the cost of international postage.

THE
GAIA DIALOGUES

Murry Hope

THOTH PUBLICATIONS

Thoth Publications
98 Ashby Road
Loughborough
Leicestershire LE11 3AF

© Murry Hope, 1995
All rights reserved

First Published 1995

ISBN 1 870450 183

Printed in the United Kingdom by
Booksprint, Bristol, Avon

TO DANUIH, WITH DEEPEST LOVE

ACKNOWLEDGEMENTS

My gratitude and sincere thanks to Professor Peter Stewart, M.Sc, D.Sc., F. Eng., without whose generous supply of up-to-date scientific information on the nature of consciousness I would never have become acquainted with the 'field' theory; to Cynthia Kenyon, B.A., for invaluable assistance with editing; George Curzon, B.Sc.Hons., for his scientific check and recommendations; Reader's Digest Association, Macmillan Publishing Co., and Element Books Ltd., for the use of extracts and illustrations from their publications; and to all those keen students and lovers of Gaia who have supplied me with the mountain of press clippings relevant to the subject matter of this book.

Additional artwork by Martin Jones.

TABLE OF CONTENTS

THE GAIA DIALOGUES

PART 1

GAIA - PAST AND PRESENT

PART ONE

GAIA – PAST AND PRESENT

INTRODUCTION

The ensuing pages are concerned with the future of, and relationship with, the planet we call Earth, and the enormous range of life-forms to which she gives support and sustenance.

GAIA - THE NAME

For those unfamiliar with the name Gaia, or the full implications of the ensuing dialogues, some explanation and amplification is necessary. In recent years the name Gaia has been ascribed to the planet upon which we live by Professor Sir James Lovelock, his now world-famous Gaia Hypothesis featuring in his books: *Gaia - A New Look at Life on Earth* (1979) and *The Ages of Gaia* (1990). Lovelock conceives of Earth as a self-regulating entity to which he has applied the Greek mythological name of Gaia. The Gaia concept has now acquired a large following, many of whom subscribe to the idea that Gaia is also a fully conscious living intelligence that is fully cognitive of what is taking place on her surface. However, Lovelock himself does not appear to endow her with a form of hominid-type consciousness or feeling, but rather suggests that, since the coming of *Homo sapiens*, she has changed her nature having, through us, become awake and aware of herself via 'our sensations of wonder and pleasure, our capacity for conscious thought and speculation, our restless curiosity and drive ...'[1] This opinion is not shared by your author, who opines that it is the other way round. After all, our bodies are host to numerous organisms, but are we influenced by them, their needs, their hopes, their evolutionary thrusts? Hardly! Doubtless the acceptance or rejection of this concept is contingent upon whether one's programming encompasses the 'complexity' concept which, by its very nature, embraces both pananimism and the 'field' theory; but more of that later.

GAIA - THE MYTH

So, what prompted Lovelock to choose the name Gaia? A dip into the informative annals of Greek mythology might possibly supply us with a few clues. According to Hesiod, in the beginning there was Chaos, vast and dark. Then appeared Gaia, the deep-breasted Earth and, finally, Eros 'the love which softens hearts', whose fructifying influence would thenceforth preside over the formation of beings and things. From Chaos were born Erebus and Night who, uniting, gave birth in their turn to Ether and Hemera, the day. On her part Gaia first bore Uranus, the sky crowned with stars 'whom she made her equal in grandeur, so that he entirely covered her'. Then she created the high mountains and Pontus, 'the sterile sea', with its harmonious waves.[2]

The universe having been formed, all that remained was for the gods to people it, so Gaia united with her son, Uranus, and produced the first race - the Titans, of which there were twelve, six male and six female. However, she also gave birth to a host of other beings, the size, shape and appearance of which Uranus regarded with horror. So much did these ugly offspring offend him that, much to Gaia's horror, he shut them away in the depths of the Earth. At first she mourned their absence but her sorrow slowly gave way to anger and she planned a terrible revenge against her husband. From her bosom she drew forth gleaming steel which she fashioned into a sickle or *harpe* and, gathering her remaining children around her, she told them of her plan. All bar one were struck with horror and refused to have any part in the dastardly deed; only the astute Cronus, her last-born, volunteered to help her. So, when evening fell and the weary Uranus, accompanied by Night, retired to his wife's side, Cronus, who had lain in hiding in his mother's bedchamber, set upon his father and castrated him, casting the bleeding genitals into the sea. The black blood that dropped from the terrible wound duly seeded both earth and water, resulting in the birth of the redoubtable Furies, monstrous giants, the ash-tree nymphs, the Meliae, and the beautiful Aphrodite.

Gaia's original oracle at Delphi was latterly reallocated to Apollo, although her gift of foretelling the future was always upheld by both gods and men, and it remained the custom among both to invoke her when effecting oaths.

What we are basically dealing with here is a mythologized version of the events which took place, following the creation of our planet and the earliest experimental-type life-forms which graced her surface. Cronus is, of course, Time, to which, it would seem, the originators of the Greek myths, in common with the Egyptian sages, ascribed a specific personality.

HER MANY NAMES

The Earth consciousness which, thanks to Lovelock, has now generally assumed the Gaia tag has, however, enjoyed many other identities over the millennia. To the ancient Egyptians she was a masculine entity whom they referred to as Geb, while those places colonized by Atlantean settlers tended to employ etymological derivatives of her old Atlantean nomenclature, Danuih (pronounced Dan-oo-ee). These may be evidenced in the myth of the Tuatha de Danaans (children of the goddess Dana or Danu) in Ireland, Dôn in Wales, Demeter and Danae in Greece, Danuna and Danu in Egypt and Northern Syria (whose people referred to her followers as 'the Peoples from the Sea') and many other variations of that nomenclature all along the Atlantic seaboard. The *Thesmophoria*, one of the great Greek Festivals associated with the Eleusinia which was celebrated in the month of October, was believed to date back to the daughters of Danaus who imported it firstly from Egypt and, prior to that, from 'a land across the ocean'. Following the Indo-Aryan invasions from the north and the decline of the matriarchal religion (Hesiod's 'Silver Age'), Danu became masculinized in some traditions as Donner, Dan, Danaus, and so forth.

Having made our acquaintance with she who affords us our homelands, let us together embark on a journey into her consciousness, so that she may share with us her feelings about her own body and her attitude towards both her natural progeny and those who, over the millions of years that have constituted part of her life-cycle to date, she has fostered for the furtherance of their somatic and spiritual evolution.

ENDNOTES:

(1) *Complexity*, Roger Lewis. Phoenix Paperbacks, p.11.
(2) *Larousse Encyclopedia of Mythology*, p.89.

Chapter 1

THE 'FIELD' THEORY

In order to understand my personal involvement with Gaia and how this came about it is necessary that I explain my own studies concerning the nature of consciousness which led me to embrace, and further develop, the 'field' theory. Although the 'field' concept could be condensed into a simple sentence - *consciousness is a field of active particles begging organization* - from the layman's point of view this says very little, if anything, of the complexities involved. A more concise description might refer to it as a creative force or field, itself composed of many particles. And yet each particle utilized for conscious expression is in itself conscious, albeit in a lesser or lesser aware degree.

Certain branches of science have recently become preoccupied with investigating consciousness. Willis W. Harman, of the Institute of Noetic Sciences, Sausalito, California, comments:

'Attempts to scientifically explore consciousness have been consistently disappointing because researchers have tended to fit their inquiries into the accepted epistemology or "scientific method," rather than boldly set out to find an epistemology appropriate to the subject of investigation. The epistemology, or set of "rules of evidence" accepted within Western science has been extraordinarily effective in achieving the goals of prediction, control, and generation of manipulative technology. However, the epistemologies of neuroscience, or cognitive science, or quantum physics are not suited to the exploration of consciousness...'

'... consciousness is not a thing to be studied by an observer who is somehow apart from it; consciousness involves the interaction of the observer, or if you like, the *experience* of observing... to be a competent investigator, the researcher must be *willing to risk being profoundly changed* through the process of exploration.'[1]

In viewing consciousness within the 'field' context, however, we have to consider that fields come in all shapes and forms, electric, magnetic, gravitational; the former, for example, being described as the space surrounding an electric charge within which it is capable of exerting a perceptible force on another electric charge[2]. The Russian scientist Alexander Gurwitsch (1874-1954) introduced the field theory into biology, postulating that consciousness (the psychic sphere in general) was a vectorial biological field. Since his death, however, the field theory has acquired far more metaphysical connotations which look good in the light of quantum theory. For example, Professor John Archibald Wheeler described consciousness as a quantum factor, only one particle of which is actually manifested in the human body, the remaining particle/wave packets residing in that delightfully vague area defined by science as 'non-locality'! This being the case, Wheeler argued, other aspects of the 'self' or one's consciousness could be experiencing simultaneously in any period of time either past or future! Reincarnation in a nutshell without the limiting encumbrance of linear time!

Physicist and Information scientist Terry Edwards adds yet another dimension to the field theory in his concept of consciousness as a non-local field which employs energies of a lower density through which to gather information. The more information gathered, the wider or broader the field and, therefore, the greater its capacity to encroach upon other fields and draw upon their knowledge, experience and databanks. It should also be borne in mind, however, that matter is but one of the many terminals for the expression of consciousness that is, in turn, created by that consciousness. I shall be dealing with this aspect in greater depths during the Gaia Dialogues which will follow in later chapters.

Edwards also emphasizes his idea of consciousness as distinct from *awarenesss*. He writes :

'It becomes necessary to define certain concepts to further these arguments: one is *consciousnesss* which becomes the capacity to sustain a conceptual pattern of existence in a consistent and meaningful form; the other is *awarenesss*, the capacity of an organism to register and utilise activity within itself and its environment for the purpose of prolonging the existence of itself and of any hierarchy to which it belongs. On the basis of these definitions biological organisms have consciousness as a brain function and so would the universe. Awareness, however, is a function of the mind and brain and there is no reason at the moment to believe that the universe shares that.' [3]

My own observations oblige me to differ from Edwards as regards the latter sentence, the *awarenesss* he defines surely equating with individuation, or the severance from the group consciousness which enables the psyche to become cognizant of the consciousness/life force in *all* existence, and not merely that identifiable with its immediate environment. For example, Lovelock's assumption that Gaia, although self regulating, is unaware by Edward's definition of the term, might certainly appear correct if viewed from the limited perspective of hominid group consciousness. However, the majority of humanity doubtless fall far short of 'individuation' as conceived by Jung, let alone its metaphysical equivalent which demands even greater sensitivity to, and understanding of, *all* things (pananimism). Gaia's awareness, like our own, is surely linked to the band-width of her field. Her critics may complain of the havoc caused to life on Earth by her self-regulating habits which appear to take place regardless of the resultant suffering, but how many of them (or any of us, come to that) make a point of consulting every life-form which lives on their body before effecting a decision which will doubtless disturb their overall physical or mental balance?

THE ROLE OF THE BRAIN

After defining consciousness as 'a field of energy in a higher dimension of space which co-exists in three-dimensional space with the human brain', Professor Peter Stewart, to whom I am deeply indebted for myriad current scientific material on this subject which he travels world-wide to collect, categorizes the triune nature of the brain in three modes: the instinctual (emanating from the reptilian brain); the emotional (as being handled by the limbic system), and the neo cortex (accommodating the right and left hemispheres and pre-frontal lobe) which he views as 'a relatively new development in evolutionary terms '. A simpler classification currently favoured by psychologists designates the right and left hemispheres and hindbrain as related to the Intuitive, Rational and Instinctive complex.

Evidence would seem to suggest that the brain itself is nothing more than a computer, albeit a complex one, which relies upon external stimuli for its programme. Such programming can emanate from the field or, when the neuronal connections with the field are weak, from:

(a) The group or race consciousness of the species.

(b) The personal genetic information encoded in the DNA.

(c) Current environmental programming.

Thus both the Nature and Nuture aspects often disputed by sociologists are jointly accommodated, although one or other may often be seen to dominate depending, no doubt, on the amount of influence exercised by the field.

THE FIELD THEORY IN PSYCHOLOGY AND METAPHYSICS

A question which naturally arises is how the field relates to the three aspects of the Self - The Instinctive, Rational and Intuitive complex, the Shadow naturally falling into the first category.

(a) The Instinctive would relate to the stratum directly below the one just attained to, or the zone from which the field has recently emerged (in metaphysical parlance, the residue of those denser or less cosmically aware levels from which the evolving spirit or soul has graduated).

(b) The Rational is, of course, the Self which observes the universe via the eyes of the body, hence the Observer Effect, which I shall deal with shortly, and the Anthropic Principle so lovingly espoused by astro-physicists.

(c) The Instinctive relates to the field itself (Higher Self metaphysically), which exists in non-locality and is comprised of a conglomerate of particles which continue to accrete (the process of expansion). However, how much of the whole field we are able to access at any one time would appear to be decided by a kind of ring-pass-not imposed by the karmic blueprint. This phenomenon has also been observed in science where it was dubbed The Principle of the Conservation of Order by the Indian physicist Ramakrishna Rao.

The balanced functioning of all three levels is essential to the maintenance of the chaos/order sequence, the Instinctive providing the terminal crucial to the earthing of the energies encountered in each cycle.

PROBLEMS OF DESIRE

Experimental psychology has shown that if a need, wish or desire is very high, behaviour becomes disorganized and performance breaks down. In quantum terms, disorder in our minds results in chaotic patterns in the particles surrounding us with which we either directly or indirectly interact. Gurwitsch's researches led him to the conclusion that thoughts were things in that they emit random particles with every thought-pattern; he refers to '...*an incessant stream of chaotic thoughts which is a certain background for all other physical activities.*'[4]

Here we have a typical example of the brain inhibiting the flow of energy from the field or, in psychological terms, a conflict between the conscious desire nature and the unconscious needs. We do, in fact, waste energy which could, with a little mental discipline, be put to more constructive use.

INTELLIGENCE AND CONSCIOUSNESS

Does intelligence relate to consciousness, or can it serve as an indicator as to the band-width of the field? Experts assure us that there is little, if any, relationship between right-brain intuition (creativity) and left brain logical intelligence. Parapsychologists noted that MENSA types with very high IQ often displayed low psi owing, no doubt, to rational interference. Intelligence as such would appear to be dictated by the brain capacity rather than the field band-width and several scientists with whom I have conversed on this subject, including one Nobel Prize Winner, have assured me that their most original and enlightened ideas have resulted not so much from methodological research techniques as from sudden flashes of right-brain intuition.

Psychologists assure us that intelligence is not a singular variable, the evidence pointing to the fact that it is hierarchical (of graded order) composed of different component skills which, for the sake of convenience, are lumped together as 'intelligence'. Experimentation has also highlighted the fact that creativity and psi are not synonymous any more than meditation is synonymous with intuition, different brain-waves being employed for each specific function.

A brilliant scientific paper relevant to this discussion has recently come into my hands via the generous offices of Professor Peter Stewart. The contributor is Professor Jacobo Grinberg-Zylberbaum of the *Universidad Nacional Autonoma de Mexico and Instituto Nacional Para el Estudio de la Conciencia* who writes:

'Reality is perceived as a result of a decodification performed by the brain upon the pre-space structure and as such involves an interpretation performed by the brain-mind apparatus.

'In general terms, every interpretation involves the transformation of a process into a discrete structure. A good example of this transformation is the feeling of the ego as a concrete mental object arising when the brain finds the algorithm that describes an ongoing and ever-changing process of brain activity. A similar operation explains the perception of an object (a rock, for example) arising when the brain computes a coherent pattern. The pattern is interpreted as an object and is projected to an exterior realm.

'The perception of the existence of an exterior realm is also an interpretation. If this interpretation is modified, the difference between exterior and interior might be dissolved. The interpretation of reality is a collective endeavour. We have shown that brain to brain interactions exist so whatever is experienced by a human being is influenced by the activity of other beings with whom an interaction has happened.

'Perception arises when an interaction between the pre-space structure and the brain occurs. The brain activates an interactional matrix called the "neuronal field" that unifies brain activity. The neuronal field interacts with the pre-space structure and from this interaction a percept is built.

'The pre-space structure is a holographic, non-local lattice that has as a basic characteristic the attribute of consciousness. The neuronal field distorts this lattice and activates a partial interpretation of it that is perceived as an image. Only when the brain-mind system is free from interpretations, do the neuronal field and pre-space structure become identical. In this situation, the perception of reality is unitary, without ego and with a lack of any duality. In this situation, pure consciousness and a feeling of an all embracing unity and luminosity is perceived.'

After telling us that in order to experience this enlightened aspect of the non-local we need to drop all pre-conceived ideas and programmes he adds:

'If the interaction takes place in the pre-space structure, we will not be able to measure any delay between the evoked and the transferred potential, thus showing the existence of non-locality as a characteristic of consciousness.'

In other words, energies brought to the earthly level from fields of pure light-energy react immediately; long periods of meditation, or lengthy sessions of healing, are not necessary if the neuronal contact with the field is exact.

This lack of neuronal/field coordination may be evidenced in the work of parapsychologist Rex Stanford. His PMIR (Psi-

Mediated Instrumental Response) theory suggests that there is no such thing as a coincidence. Events are manipulated subconsciously all the time without the conscious attention of the individual concerned. And this also goes for our general health, reaction to stress factors, wishes, needs and desires all of which, no doubt, is orchestrated from or by the field.

Computer terminology serves us well in respect of the field theory, a familiarity with the correct passwords (access codes) being essential to the acquisition of knowledge external to the immediate field environment. In metaphysical terms we are, of course, referring to soul-age, the more mature soul-fragment having access to cosmic information only denied to younger psyches by their lack of visionary breadth or the circumscribed programmes imposed upon them during the formative stages of their physical development.

FIELD INTERACTION

In the light of the aforegoing the question which naturally arises is: can anyone's field (consciousness) interact with other fields, possibly of an entirely different nature or complexity, in order to gain knowledge of the development processes undertaken and knowledge (information) thus gained by those fields? It would appear not, field interaction access potential being decided by:

1. The brain's computorial range (number of megabytes available, etc.).

2. The band-width of the field.

Access codes to more informed terminals can be acquired either in the physical worlds or non-locality. However, contrary to the views of some, there are no short cuts whatsoever to the attaining of this knowledge which is neither there for the buying nor taking; it has to be earned in other, more subtle, ways.

Relative to the above, the continuing extention of consciousness which we call evolution could be likened to the growth of a child: in its infancy and teenage it is dominated by the less conscious (less informed in field terms) frequencies of physical matter it is utilizing (runs wild), being unable to distinguish chaos from order, destruction from construction, etc. (although, according to certain mystical teachings it, is faced with this option at *many points along its evolutionary journey*). People tend to respond to positive or negative cosmic currents or invading fields according to the nature and band-width of their own field. For the undiscerning, chaotic contacts are conducive to destruction and fragmentation whereas the more discerning are able to utilize the chaotic experience to add wisdom to their memory banks.

The compatibility factor also needs to be taken into consideration, certain fields, like certain chemicals, being incompatible to the extent that interaction between them results in chaos. In human terms there are those people with whom we feel totally at ease and whose company we benefit from, the feeling being mutual, and others who seem to exert a destructive effect on our lives at any of several levels (practical, emotional or spiritual).

ACCESSING THE MEMORY-BANKS OF NON-HOMINID ENTITIES

What do we mean by 'non-hominid'? Much as it may bruise the ego of mankind there are numerous other fields of consciousness with which we share the bosom of Gaia, as well as an infinite number of life-forms, each carrying a varying quotient of consciousness, external to this planet, both in particle form and non-locality. The process of accessing non-hominid fields is, of course, made easier if the field of the enquirer originated in the evolutionary stream of the consciousness in question. The fact that one wears a hominid body in the 'now' should never be taken as an indication that one's field originated within that species. Primitive shamanism offers a simple example of field access to other life-forms which, in turn, may provide easier access to, say, a planetary field.

TIMELESSNESS IN NON-LOCALITY

Since the field exists in non-locality it has access to timelessness, although either its personal ring-pass-not (see below), or its cerebral programming may preclude it from decoding information gained therefrom. Instances of Multidimensional Awareness - the ability to compute mentally more than one state of reality, or time frequency, simultaneously - are not uncommon, however, although they are mostly related to the frequencies of this universe. (Your author views Time as an energy in its own right, but more of that later.)

THE 'BELIEF' FACTOR

Since the band-width of the field constitutes a determining factor in our understanding of events or conditions external to our immediate environment, those of us who are less conscious (younger souls) will inevitably have difficulty computing any form of information that the field has not yet encountered. This does, of course, account for the fact that, although evidence of a concrete nature is presented to some people, they are unable to accept it or, perhaps, too frightened to so do. Religious programming can also exert a restricting effect on the expression of consciousness in that the accepted programme offers a sense of moral and spiritual security which the brain is reluctant to relinquish.

Equally damaging to both the brain/consciousness relationship and the field theory credibility factor is the accelerating bandwaggon of supposed 'channelling', ninety-nine point nine, nine, nine per cent of which is based on information immediate to the surroundings of the channeller. I shall be dealing with the channelling phenomenon later and, incidentally, I DO NOT channel as such.

THE MASTER CONSCIOUSNESS THEORY

Religious thinking inevitably intrudes into the field theory, some believers turning to computer technology to explain the idea of a Master Consciousness which can only be accessed via a series of complex terminals. In other words there is no immediate hot line to God as such because when we pray the stream of particles emitted by the request will only reach those terminals which the field is programmed to handle. As the field expands (we become older souls), so access codes to more powerful terminals become available and, with such exalted connections, the knowledge naturally flows. However, as a computer, the human brain also has its limitations, with which it will be lumbered until the next quantum leap when its DNA will be mutated by the ensuing surge of radioactivity culminating in the activation of hitherto unused areas. This will result in a far wider field of knowledge and experience being made available to the rational Self via the expanded field.

THE FIELD v. 'THE SUBTLE BODIES'?

For centuries metaphysicists and mystics have harboured the notion of a series of subtle bodies which, they assure us, are essential to our negotiation of those planes of existence beyond the immediate. Sorry, but the field theory does rather tend to dismiss such concepts which are, after all, simply mirror images emitted by the left brain in its efforts to rationalize the abstract. The field itself is simply energy. The only shape it can manifest once it is free of the body is that imposed by the programming it receives during any specific life. I view these so-termed 'bodies' as computer-like images projected on to the field by the currently functioning cerebral programming. As far as consciousness is concerned, the terminology applied to such 'vehicles' simply relates to the mode adopted by the field when negotiating other frequencies to which it has access.

However, it must always be borne in mind that, while conscious elements from faster frequencies are able to negotiate denser regions, the opposite does not apply, and connections with higher levels of consciousness from exalted wavebands can only result from a joint effort on both sides. One is reminded of the fact that a photon can behave as a wave in one space and a particle in another, which rather suggests that fields capable of negotiating the higher frequencies of light are also able to move into denser areas in order to draw information from, or relate knowledge to, intelligences within those strata.

GHOSTLY PHENOMENA?

Fields caught in time-warps (ghosts!) tend to exhibit the appearance of the soma associated with the life which has contributed to its predicament, the cause of which is usually a highly emotional death-sequence which tends to leave the final imprint of the physical brain on the field until it is released. Raising the frequency surrounding the entrapped field (soul) will inevitably release it from any time-warp, in much the same way that a magnetic tape is cleaned for reprogramming. It does well to remember that we are all subject to the forces of T.O.E. (Theory of Everything, formerly known as the Grand Unified Theory), these being the Weak and Strong Nuclear Forces, the Electromagnetic Fields, Gravity and that enigmatic unifying Force (still undiscovered by science but dubbed the Higgs Force after Professor Higgs of Edinburgh University) which I, in the company of several scientists considerably more learned than myself, have designated as Time.

THE OBSERVER EFFECT

If you, the reader, are beginning to feel somewhat overwhelmed by a surfeit of science please bear with me because, without these explanations, my Gaia experience could not be adequately explained or accounted for. Besides, I have been privileged to access a lot of it from her own memory banks and she is of the opinion that it is about time that humanity dropped the two extremes of dialectic materialism and religiosity and faced up to the real facts.

Scientists have long known that the act of observing a state causes it to change, the choice of an observer to measure a particular property of a system literally forcing that system from a probable state to an actual one. In the world of quantum mechanics, that which the metaphysicist would view as etheric, or not of this world, is referred to as 'fuzzy', or relating to the wave aspect of a particle/wave packet; the particle is the part you can see when you look, whereas the wave resides with all the other 'fuzzies' in that delightfully vague area known scientifically as non-locality (it could be anywhere in any universe!).

Fuzzy systems, however, become discrete *when they are observed* or, in the language of the physicist, a particle only acquires velocity when we measure it. Prior to that it is non-local or a 'wave'. However, an observer must also prepare the state of the system before he or she observes it, hence the saying 'Seeing is believing, believing is seeing!' In other words, we subliminally programme the abstract so that it inevitably turns out to be what we expect. This fact of science is manifestly obvious in the area of parapsychology dealing with psychic research, wherein one encounters one particular aspect of the Experimenter Effect (see below).

THE UNSEEN IS EVER PRESENT

Just because you can't see it does not mean that it isn't there! Professor Stephen Hawking tells us:

'The force-carrying particles exchanged between matter particles are said to be "virtual" particles because, unlike "real" particles, they cannot be detected directly by a particle detector. We know they exist, however, because they do have a measurable effect: they give rise to forces between matter particles. Particles of spin 0, 1 or 2 do also exist in some circumstances as real particles, when they can be directly detected. They then appear to us as what classical physicists would call waves, such as waves of light or gravitational waves. They may sometimes be emitted when matter particles interact with each other by exchanging virtual force-carrying particles. (For example, the electric repulsive force between two electrons is due to the exchange of virtual photons, which can never be directly detected; but if one electron moves past another, real photons may be given off, which we detect as light waves.)' [5]

Likewise there is the now famous 'dark matter' of which astrophysicists and astronomers seem to believe (for the time being, anyway!) much of the universe is composed. You certainly cannot see it, but sensitive instrumentation can detect its presence because of its light-bending qualities. If one translates all this information into consciousness/field terms, it makes sense of much of the more profound metaphysical teachings.

THE EXPERIMENTER EFFECT

The Experimenter Effect is a useful piece of knowledge to have at one's finger-tips, methodological research having established that the beliefs, feelings and inclinations of the experimenter, or person undertaking the experiment, are the deciding factor as to the experiment's outcome. (Ref: *Explaining the Unexplained* by Professor Hans Eysenck and Dr.Carl Sargent.) Musing along ring-pass-not lines, one supposes that when people are ready for the information they will cause the experiment to yield up the proof!

THE ANTHROPIC PRINCIPLE

Beloved of the materialistic school of astro-physics, the Anthropic Principle could be viewed as a sort of universal extension of the Observer Effect. It is necessary that I mention it at this stage or some of the information contained in the ensuing Dialogues will not make much sense. The Anthropic Principle postulates that the universe is there because we are here to observe it; without us it would not exist. I now add my corollary to that: we observe it because it functions at the same frequency as our physical bodies. Other universes which coexist within and around our own are not observable unless we either slow down or quicken our perceptive faculties. Strangely enough, quantum worlds are unreal worlds in the light of currently accepted standards of logic in that they do not conform to the Laws of Matter to which we have become accustomed (programmed!).

Working with an extended field, or via the fields of more exalted energies, one can gain a greater perspective of the nature and purpose of interwoven universes, all of which serves to support the complexity principle as against currently favoured reductionist approaches. My own mental journeys have taken me to the subatomic worlds where the minutest of particles assume viewable proportions, and to universes further up the scale, where what we see as astronomic is microscoped to the diminutive when viewed from a faster frequency. All very interesting but, sadly, such knowledge only tends to highlight how little one knows, one's place as a minute particle/wave packet in an infinite universe becoming more and more apparent.

And now to more of Gaia.

ENDNOTES:

(1) Harman, W. W. *A Comparison of Three Approaches To the Problem of Science and Consciousnesss.* (The IV International Symposium on Science and Consciousness, Uxmal, Yucatan, Mexico, 4-8 January, 1994.)
(2) *Dictionary of Physics*, p.121.
(3) Edwards, T. *Quantum Domains, Chaos & The Theory of Fractogenesis,* p. 6.
(4) *Analysis of the Physical Sphere Manifestations by the Theory of the Biological Field,* by A. G. Gurwitsch. Trans. Michael Lipkind, University of Israel.
(5) Hawking, Stephen. *A Brief History of Time*, p. 69.

Chapter 2

GAIA'S BODY

A QUESTION OF AGE

Before we can contemplate, or even try to comprehend, Gaia's personal field, some knowledge of her soma is essential. And, since we are dealing with the evolutionary pattern of a cosmic body akin to other such phenomena we view in our night sky, a consideration of the overall age of that physical universe might serve to give us an idea of her position in relation to her own cosmic kind.

The universe with which we are directly connected is estimated as being some five thousand million years old and still growing. In the beginning, we are told, it was hot and symmetrical, now it is cold and asymmetrical (water, when running warm, is symmetrical but when cold, as in a snowflake, it is asymmetrical). However, astronomers have recently claimed the discovery of a globular cluster (47 Tucanal) seventeen billion years old; but perhaps we should wait for further confirmation of this before adjusting our text-books. Likewise, astronomers have noted our own galaxy seems to be veering towards the constellation of Virgo, as though being pulled by some invisible force (dark matter, perhaps?), while a smaller galaxy appears to be slowly impinging on its frontiers. Viewed in the microcosm/macrocosm context, however, surely the behaviour of galaxies is no different from that of particles, size being determined by perspective. When viewed from a faster frequency universe our seemingly immense display would probably appear as no more than a conglomerate of chaotic particles striving for organization. In other words, the pattern is identical in all creation from the

The Great Attraction

As the universe expands in all directions, our own galaxy seems to be veering towards the constellation of Virgo.

Virgo

Milky way

500 million light years

THE UNIVERSE

Only a truly massive body would have the gravitational pull to cause this. But what is it and where is it?

The Lauer/Postman survey was the largest observation of its kind to date, stretching 500 million light years into space.

Not drawn to scale

GRAPHIC: PADDY ALLEN/ TIM RADFORD

Dark matter

The speed at which stars and gas clouds move around the outer edges of the galaxies suggest that there is 10 or even 100 times as much 'dark' or invisible matter as there is in all the stars together.

Gravity

The bigger the mass of a given body; the bigger its gravitational pull. Some stars are so massive they collapse into black holes from which not even light can escape.

More mass equals more pull; the larger body drags the smaller to it.

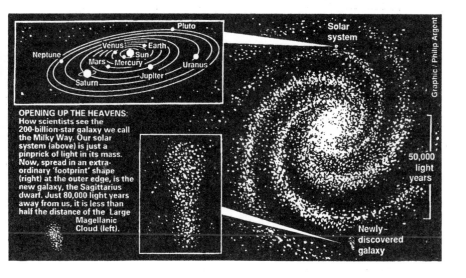

Pluto

Solar system

Neptune

Venus Earth

Mars Mercury Sun

Jupiter Uranus

Saturn

Graphic / Philip Argent

OPENING UP THE HEAVENS: How scientists see the 200-billion-star galaxy we call the Milky Way. Our solar system (above) is just a pinprick of light in its mass. Now, spread in an extra-ordinary 'footprint' shape (right) at the outer edge, is the new galaxy, the Sagittarius dwarf. Just 80,000 light years away from us, it is less than half the distance of the Large Magellanic Cloud (left).

50,000 light years

Newly-discovered galaxy

Illustrations from *The Guardian*, March 22, 1994.
& *Daily Mail*, April 6, 1994.

largest to the smallest, either end stretching way beyond the present computing ability of our somewhat limited brains.

But to return to Gaia. Taking into account the geological age of her body as illustrated below, the various epochs that have constituted her history to date and the evolutionary quantum leaps that have taken place during those eras, it would seem obvious to assume that she is a fully mature entity probably nearing, or even about to embark upon, the final stage of her evolutionary cycle.

THE BIRTH OF GAIA

Gaia was born, or so science tells us, some 4600 million years ago, the formation of her crust, the continents and the oceans taking place during the Pre-Cambrian era (see diagram).

From the aforegoing we may see that Gaia has been around a long time by our reckoning, during which many different species have come and gone on her surface prior to the advent of *Homo sapiens*, humankind representing more of a final phase in her evolutionary cycle than the culmination of an earlier one. I also detect the kind of acceleration of chaos (entropy) indicative of the approaching end of a cycle prior (we hope) to the eventual return to a new sequence of order. Or is that a pipe-dream?

Judging Gaia's evolutionary progress against the analogy of the triple Goddess - Maiden, Mother and Crone - she appears to have approached that age, both in body and soul, particle and wave, field and matter, or whichever concept of her beingness you may care to accord credence to, where she is about to accept the role of the latter. I can tell you more of this when dealing with my personal experiences with her. It is humankind, not Gaia, which is still in the bloom of youth (infanthood or childhood in many cases!), which is why she will need to undertake a gigantic sort-out before she can proceed to her next term of experience in the university of her physical body.

But to return to her physical youth: as may be seen from the above diagram there was a period in her early history, some two-hundred million years ago, when all the continents of the world were grouped together in a single landmass, which is known in geology as Pangaea (from the Greek word meaning 'all earth'). At the end of the Palaeozoic era, Pangaea split into two sections,

HOW LIFE HAS EVOLVED

The Earth's story, revealed by its rocks

The eras of the Earth have been well established by isotope dating in which the age of rocks is determined by the amount of radioactive-decay products they contain. Major divisions reflect changes in the positions of continents and the emergence of new forms of life.

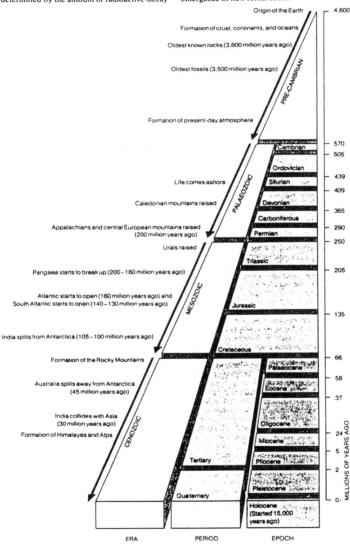

ERAS OF THE WORLD *Eras (and periods) are defined by life forms. Fossils in pre-Cambrian rocks are very rare. The Palaeozoic ("old life") saw the rise of invertebrates and amphibians. The Mesozoic ("middle life") was the age of reptiles. The Cenozoic ("recent life") is the age of mammals.*

Illustration from *Reader's Digest*
Great Illustrated Dictionary, page 700. (see previous page)

THE LAYERS OF THE EARTH
Earthquakes reveal the mystery of the Earth's interior

Although the Earth's interior cannot be studied directly, the measurement of earthquake waves as they bend through it has revealed three major layers.

The outermost layer of the planet is the crust (upper layer) beneath which lies the mantle (middle layer) and the core (lower layer). The place of contact between the crust and mantle is called the Mohorovičić discontinuity (Moho for short). As earthquake waves cross from the crust to the mantle, they increase in speed by 15 per cent.

The crust is divided into two types, the oceanic and continental, and the mantle is divided into upper and lower regions with a transition zone between. Around the solid inner core there is a fluid outer core, in which the circulation of electrical currents causes the Earth's magnetic field.

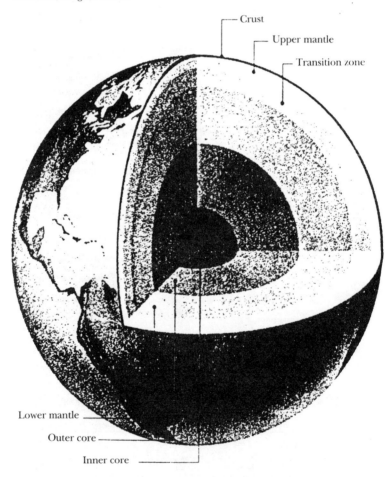

Crust

Upper mantle

Transition zone

Lower mantle

Outer core

Inner core

Illustration from *Reader's Digest*
Great Illustrated Dictionary, page 528.

Gondwanaland, which is the name ascribed to the hypothetical southern portion which consisted of Africa, South America, India, Arabia, Australia, Madagascar, New Guinea, the Malay Peninsular, Indonesia and Antarctica; and Lurasia, the northern portion, which comprised North America, Greenland, Europe and Asia (excluding the Indian subcontinent). Lurasia itself split, during the Mesozoic era, into North America and Europe.

The German zoologist Ernst Haeckel saw Gondwanaland as being synonymous with the legendary continent of Lemuria, although it is more likely that the Lemuria or Mu of myth was much smaller and probably lay in the region of, or near, the west coast of South America; from where, possibly, it linked with a chain of islands which spanned the Pacific allowing access to mariners between South America and the Far East. Evidence to this effect may be seen in the similarity in dress, culture and physical appearance between certain Indian races still extant in South America and those of the inhabitants of China, Mongolia and Tibet in particular. However, all this constitutes another study which is well covered in my book *Atlantis: Myth or Reality?*

THE ANATOMY AND PHYSIOLOGY OF GAIA

Science has afforded us a great deal of information regarding the actual body of Gaia, details of which are explicitly shown below.

Just as our fields gather information from the experiences undergone by our bodies so Gaia also expands her field-knowledge through the workings of her internal structures. However, it does not stop there; she is also able to expand her consciousness (field) through the negotiation of not only her elemental brethren, the forces of which her form is constituted, but also via an awareness of ALL the life forms which occupy her space. In other words, she has learned, and is still learning, to understand the hominid species along with all else to which she offers sustenance and an opportunity to evolve both somatically and spiritually.

A comparison with our own stage of evolutionary development as a species, as against Gaia's age and experience, is surely a clear indicator of how far humankind has yet to go before its awareness faculty is sufficiently developed to encompass, and therefore feel for and with, the myriad minute life-forms which exist on our bodies. After all, the majority of people occupying space on Gaia's body today fail even to acknowledge her existence as an entity in her own right, let alone consider the rights, feelings, hopes and fears of what are seen as 'less intelligent life forms'. Some of the major religions of today still preach the erroneous doctrine of the supremacy of the hominid species, their cosmic racist and speciesist dogmas choosing to ignore the fact that every *thing* - be it animal, vegetable or mineral - is conscious to a greater or lesser degree. This consciousness may not equate with our idea of intelligence but then who are we to judge? And in the final analysis it will be Gaia who has the last say because, for all our pride, we are no match for her power or that of her cosmic family who will doubtless assist her through her forthcoming rite of passage.

THE HOMININNAE

Perhaps we should take a brief look at our own species as related to the overall somatic and spiritual development of Gaia. The subject of the evolution of *Homo sapiens* has long been a contentious issue, the word *hominoid* (hominid is more popularly used these days) referring to the superfamily *Hominoidea*. Recent studies of genetic fingerprinting have, however, added new dimensions to our understanding of our relationship with the animals with which we share this planet, the anthropological implications being dramatic. It has now been established that the human, chimp and gorilla all share a common ancestry as recently as five million years ago. Humans, it seems, are more closely akin to chimpanzees than either humans or chimps are to gorillas. Only one per cent of our DNA differs from that of chimps. Certain anthropologists, notably Morris Goodman of Wayne State University, have therefore proposed that humans, chimps and gorillas should now be placed in the same new sub-family, *Homininnae*, instead of leaving humans in proud isolation within their own classification.

However, as so often occurs in the field of scientific research, new information regarding that enigmatic evolutionary missing link between apes and humans has now surfaced in the form of a skeleton recently discovered in the Ethiopian desert which has been nicknamed 'Lucy'. Anthropologists were puzzled at first by the fact that Lucy appeared to conform to the chimpanzee in all respects except her legs, the knee joints of which were decidedly human. This suggested that she and her kind walked upright, possibly driven to so adapt by the changing face of the environment. Darwinists would doubtless quote this as proof of their evolutionist theories but there is another answer which lies not only in the quantum leaps of individual particles but also in those of the planet herself and, therefore, all that dwells thereon. How these quantum leaps are effected by an interplay between Gaia and some, as yet unknown, external cosmic force, will be covered in a later chapter.

IMPLICATE AND EXPLICATE ORDER

In his book *Wholeness and the Implicate Order* (1980) the late Professor David Bohm postulated that the universe is defined or described at every 'point' of space by a regime he refers to as implicate order. Bohm's idea is basically that all things, human beings included, should not be viewed simply as a collection of atoms but as a unified concept defined abstractly and expressed in molecular form. Terry Edwards refers to:

'... a collection of molecules having conveniently useful and randomly generated properties ... Underlying you is the concept of human life and underlying that is the concept of life on this planet; nothing should be seen as separate from the whole and the planet is an expression of a particular life pattern. (If another planet exists in the universe having a biology of a similar nature then our mutual developments are inexplicably entwined irrespective of distance.) ... The sequence of implicate to explicate (concept - geometric translation - fractal pattern - emergent structure) is the process by which I believe Sheldrake's metamorphic resonance occurs. The matrix is the medium in which the output of the processing is "displayed"; other matrices may represent alternative outlets or other virtual realities'. [1]

Now I am no scientist as such (although I rather like to think of myself as a metaphysicist who has crept into science through the back door) but the above seems to suggest two things to me, firstly, the parallel world theory and secondly the EPR Paradox. The first of these receives excellent coverage in *Parallel Universes - the search for other worlds*, by theoretical physicist Fred Alan Wolf. The famous Einstein-Podolski-Rosen Paradox, which I have dealt with at length in my book *Time: The Ultimate Energy*, concerns the measurement performed on one part of a physical system while the other part, which had previously been connected to it, was left alone. According to quantum rules, the measured part instantly affects the unmeasured part at the moment of measurement, regardless of space-time differences. This so affronted Einstein's logic that he dubbed it 'spooky action-at-a-distance'. Think about it.

Bohm also refers to the *holomovement* - the process of unfoldment from implicate to explicate order, which must obviously take place at all levels and has probably added fuel to the reductionism v. complexity issue. Edwards continues:

> 'What the universe appears to seek is *complexity*, ever greater degrees of organisation on all things (biological, inorganic and even in more nebulous aspects of existence such as the way society organises itself and its artefacts). It is likely that what we call *instinct* is directly attributable to the Universe. A logical principle of an organic universe would be the avoidance of repetition and exact duplication as far as possible in all things, especially of form and experience. It is not logically consistent with the idea that the universe operates on a basis of uniformity and structure of property throughout, that living organisms could exist without registering the fact of that existence on the processes that enable these things.' [2]

Enlightened and more logically motivated metaphysicists have long been aware of the principle of the avoidance of repetition although I, personally, find Bohms' theory, together with those of other exponents of what has come to be termed the 'New Science', infinitely more acceptable than certain religiously-orientated, outmoded mystical notions of the field's expansion resulting from experience in different streams of lower consciousness. (We start as a stone, progressing thence to the plant kingdoms and then on to the lower animals etc.) Recent research work with crystals, plants, dolphins etc. has tended to show that many of these life forms exhibit qualities of field expansion far beyond the horizon of the vast majority of mankind. In other words, the fact that their brains are not fashioned to compute information in the same way as ours should not be taken as an indication that they are spiritually lesser evolved. In fact, animals, insects, plant life, etc., either in the group or individual mode, have shown their ability to interact with Gaia's field time and time again. Interestingly enough they are also able to anticipate her approaching quantum leaps, but more of that in a later chapter.

EARTH FAILS THE INTELLIGENCE TEST

An article on astrobiology in *The Sunday Telegraph* (24 October 1993) by science editor Adrian Berry entitled *Earth Fails the Intelligence Test*, carrying the sub-heading 'Alien visitors could fail to find traces of civilisation on our planet', struck me as relevant to our subject matter. Berry tells us:

'An experiment using photographs of the Earth taken three years ago by Nasa's Galileo spacecraft from a mere 600 miles found not a single indication of the existence of intelligent life - a result that seems amazing in the light of our ever-growing technology.'

Berry continues by quoting one of the team involved, Dr. W. Reid Thompson, of Cornell University, New York, co-author of a paper in last week's *Nature*, as saying:

'If that spacecraft had been sent by a group of alien scientists from another planet, nothing in these pictures would prove to them that this world was the abode of intelligent creatures. All they show is white clouds, the blue of the oceans, and the brown outlines of South America and Australia. Neither cities nor agricultural fields can be identified as artificial objects, since their rectangular shapes are undetectable. The spacecraft might see the glint of sunlight from satellites and large aircraft, and it might observe aircraft contrails. But the "conservatives" among the alien scientists - in any scientific debate there are always "conservatives" - and radicals - could all too plausibly insist that these phenomena were merely cosmic rays striking their own detectors.'

Berry questioned:

'But what if the spacecraft photographed the planet at night (which Galileo did not)?'

The reply was:

'I think they could explain the lights of cities as natural fires or lowly phosphorescent organisms with whom it would not be worth communicating.

'Since our languages would be unintelligible to them, and perhaps not even recognisable as languages, they might even mistake our radio and television signals for natural radio activity. Similarly, the oxygen in our atmosphere might be considered, not as supportive of life but as poisonous to it.

'The moral is that we should not be too hasty to conclude that other planets and moons in the solar system, of which more than 60 have been surveyed by our spacecraft, were necessarily lifeless. When looking at other planets close up, one should always examine that extra bit of data, even if the exercise might at first seem pointless.

'For example, Saturn's giant moon, Titan, which has a rich methane atmosphere, may well contain the building blocks of life.'

Berry then goes on to tell us that the *Nature* team were radicals, and a scientist of the rival 'conservative' school would naturally disagree with their premises and produce valid arguments for so doing. Whether either we, with our so-termed 'civilization', or Gaia herself for that matter, are dismissed by visiting aliens as being of no consequence does rather speak for the limited field understanding of the visitors, however. After all, were their consciousness on a par with their advanced technology, they would simply access Gaia's memory banks and save themselves a lot of time and trouble.

All in all there is as much twaddle talked by scientists as there is by exponents of the so-termed 'New Age' and those of metaphysical inclination who insist on hanging their washing (not all of it pristine by any means!) on the clothes lines of past dogmas. While the first group cling tenaciously to their left-brain rationale and the latter appear to deny the existence of that most useful faculty, group three is no less rigid than the religious fundamentalists they delight in decrying.

Poor Gaia; what a chaotic and argumentative bunch she is landed with! Which brings to mind something I was told by a Time Lord many years ago: 'Your planet could be likened to a mental hospital in which the patients have overpowered and imprisoned the doctors and nurses, and are now indulging their insane fantasies via the contents of the drug cupboards.'

Gaia, the field, comes next.

ENDNOTES:

(1) Edwards, Terry. *Quantum Domains, Chaos, and the Theory of Fractogenesis*, pp. 4 & 8.
(2) *Ibid.*, page 6.

Chapter 3

GAIA - THE CONSCIOUSNESS

Having established that all manifestations of matter at the viewable level are subject to the influence of the field, this phenomenon must obviously apply to Gaia in the same way that it applies to each and every one of us. However, as has already been discussed, since the extent of control the field is able to bring to bear on its physical vehicle is governed by its band-width on the one hand and the ability of the brain to decode its directives on the other, variations in expression can be boundless.

Gaia's body is, of course, vastly different from our own. Likewise, her life-cycle encompasses far greater periods of time although, bearing in mind that time is relevant to (a) the nature of the vehicle utilizing its energies and (b) the time-frequency that vehicle is in the process of negotiating, what must appear as vast eras to us probably constitutes no more than a few seconds in the time-frame of her evolutionary journey. And so we have Gaia, the physical body, and Gaia, the field, which is the controlling essence behind that body.

THE PSYCHOLOGY OF GAIA

Dare we, who are undoubtedly guilty of both speciesism and cosmic racism, raise the question as to whether Gaia's psychology has any parallels with our own? Surely such a comparison is valid on the grounds that although her body does not resemble ours in volume and shape she is, like ourselves, composed principally of the element of water. In psychological terms this would suggest an intelligence whose responses to given stimuli might tend towards the emotional rather than the rational. However, in spite of her watery predominance her interior structure is fiery, her outer layer earthy and her body well aired by the winds which move restlessly across her surface. Metaphysically speaking, this would connote an entity which originated in the elemental stream as an ondine, later gaining its four-fold nature which served to elevate it to deva status. This has now been confirmed by Gaia, but more of that later.

But does Gaia, like us, also have a higher self, lower self, shadow, id, or whatever and, if so, how do these manifest at the physical level? In other words, how do they affect us? Let us first of all examine some of the more conventional psychological approaches to these aspects of the 'self' and see how they apply to Gaia. For example, does her collective unconscious bear any relationship to ours?

Sigmund Freud, designated the father of modern psychology, defined the personality as having three vital strands: the id, the ego and the super-ego, the former being totally unconscious and the latter two a mixture of conscious and unconscious. The id, sometimes referred to as the animal energy, is concerned with instinctive impulses and demands for immediate gratification of primitive needs and desires. As the boiling cauldron of the personality, it represents a strong force which often finds expression in fantasies. Being amoral, it has no sense of right and wrong; hence its association with man's darker nature. Desire, aggression and need are said to emanate from the id, and its power to affect our physical responses may be evidenced in the sexual effects of fantasizing. On the other hand, religious fantasizing has been known to produce stigmata, so I do not feel that we can necessarily allocate all somatic responses to mental stimulus to the chthonian regions.

The ego was viewed by Freud as the conscious driving force that controls the id and prevents it from having its own way, the ego only allowing the id to fulfil those desires which are not to its detriment. Following Freud's death a group of psychologists, led by his daughter Anna, broke away from his original concept, believing that the ego had its own store of energy which enabled it to satisfy its personal, social and creative needs independent of, and without constant conflict with, the id. Today, however, the term ego is more generally used to denote the 'I', or unique expression of the individuality, rather than the mind or psyche.

While Freudian psychology views the ego as a personal value system, the upper layer of the personality, or super-ego, is seen as an amalgam of belief systems based on external standards set by society, its main role being to suppress the unseemly desires of the id by forcing the ego to ignore all the id's basic urges. Its reward, should it succeed in this mission, is societal approval.

The popular use of the term 'psyche' can probably be attributed to the work of the late Carl Gustav Jung, who deviated from Freudian thinking in his belief in the collective unconscious. He called the whole personality the psyche and maintained that it has three levels: the ego, which is the conscious mind; the personal unconscious, in which is stored all our repressed fantasies, dreams and desires; and the collective unconscious, which is part of the primordial past which each of us inherits. It is from the latter that we derive our image of archetypes, which prove so important in subconscious communication and therefore exert a profound effect on our state of balance or otherwise. Jung also conceived of the 'shadow' or darker side of the self which needed to be faced up to and overcome. I feel intuitively that, were Gaia to face a Jungian analyst, she would relate more easily to the archetypal analogies and mental procedures involved than to some of the other schools of psychology popularly favoured in today's world, although I could, of course, be quite wrong.

History abounds with threefold references to the nature of human consciousness which were commonly accepted long before the advent of modern psychiatry. We have already considered the natural/instinctive, rational/intellectual and creative/intuitive, for example, while many of the gods and goddesses of early religions were viewed as triplicities, each representing a characteristic aspect of the human soul or psyche, or a specific stage in its evolutionary development. The Triple Goddess, maiden/mother/crone, is a typical example.

GAIA - THE TRIPLICITY

In daring to consider Gaia in human or near-human terms I am, perhaps, causing her some offence. But I think not, as it has ever been in the nature of hominids to seek in order to find, to ask in order to know, factors she must have been well aware of when she agreed to accept us into her 'classroom'. In Jungian terms,

Gaia's psyche would encompass her ego, her personal unconscious and her password (access code or key) to the collective unconscious. However, her collective unconscious, unlike our own, would naturally relate to the history and evolution of her own species, those fields or streams of consciousness which have been designated by metaphysicists as devic or elemental. Her databanks would therefore carry facts relative to the rest of the planets in our solar system, our Sun, and the binary stars-system from which this corner of the galaxy was seeded. These could also provide her with information relating to the evolutionary programme of her own group-psyche and, possibly, those of other species directly connected with her role in their development. Likewise, any of her own kind who have by accident or purpose landed up in hominid bodies would also be able to key-in to the databanks of her field to a greater or lesser degree depending on the band-width of their own fields.

GAIA'S SHADOW

In his famous television interview, which served to put Gaia on the map for many who had been previously unaware of her existence as a self-regulating entity, Professor Sir James Lovelock's reference to the darker side of her personality carried sinister undertones. To the psychologist this would, of course, equate with her shadow or id. But how could a planetary genius, albeit an intelligent entity such as Gaia, use her personal shadow in such a way as to be detrimental to mankind and other species existing on her body? The obvious answer to that is: 'Ask the dinosaurs; they caught a whiff of it and look what happened to them!' It is only logical to suppose that Gaia exerts some authority over both her own children and those she has elected to foster over the aeons, in much the same way as the minute life-forms which exist on our bodies are subject to our abusive and destructive whims. Since we would appear to exhibit a greater degree of consciousness than, say, the bacteria in our intestines, one could argue that our mistreatment of that area of our bodies is no cause for concern. Arrogant premises of this kind are frequently preached by those major religions which do not accord field-status (souls) to animals, or any form of sentient life. However, were Gaia to view us in much the same way, which I rather suspect that she does - some of us, anyway - we could well find ourselves careering after the dinosaurs with the proverbial boot in our rears.

THE NATURE OF THE SHADOW

Perhaps a closer look at the significance of the shadow might serve to throw some light on Gaia's reaction to the malicious and destructive practices of that unruly brood we call 'humankind', which seems to delight in desecrating her body and the bodies of other species to which she has given a temporary home. Cirlot tells us:

> 'As the Sun is the light of the spirit, so shadow is the negative "double" of the body, or the image of its evil and base side. Among primitive peoples, the notion that the shadow is the *alter ego* or soul is firmly established; it is also reflected in the folklore and literature of some advanced cultures. As Frazer has noted, the primitive often regards his shadow, or his reflection in water or in a mirror, as his soul or as a vital part of himself.' [1]

Dream analysts are prone to telling us that a mirror image seen during a dream sequence is indicative of the true 'self' minus the egotistical trappings acquired during our progress through society. Thus the shadow, and therefore its proportion in relation to our consciousness as a whole, may be perceived to our chagrin. Jung wrote:

> '... whoever looks into the mirror of the water will see first of all his own face. Whoever goes to himself risks a confrontation with himself. The mirror does not flatter, it faithfully shows whatever looks into it; namely, the face we never show to the world because we cover it with the *persona*, the mask of the actor. But the mirror lies behind the mask and shows the true face.' [2]

Popular occult fiction writers often feature among the more frightening aspects of their narratives the ancient belief that the Devil has no shadow. Surely the truth behind this superstition lies in the fact that in order to come to terms with the darker side of our nature we are obliged to acknowledge its existence as a natural manifestation of chaos in the human spirit. Deny this fact and we are as good as damned! In other words, if we cannot differentiate between good and evil (order and chaos?) we have not yet arisen from the chaotic abyss of ignorance; in field terminology our band-width is miniscule or, as the metaphysicists would say, we are very young souls indeed.

Gaia's shadow was well understood by the ancients who gave her many names in her guise as the dispenser of destruction and chaos. To the ancient Egyptians she was Sekhmet, the lioness-headed goddess who almost wiped out a whole race because it had offended her father, Ra. Likewise, to the peoples of the Indian subcontinent she was Kali, wife of Siva, who could also appear as the beautiful young Parvati, the ascetic Uma, or the dreaded Durga. Her equivalent in Celtic mythology is seen by some as The Morrigan (Ireland) or The Cailleach (Scotland). Surely the archetypes are identical? Could we be dealing here with some of the many faces of Gaia?

It would seem that we are all due for a taste of Gaia's shadow before long. But then that is to be expected if we are able to compute the scientifically accepted alternations of the chaos/ order sequence. Viewed over vast eras of time, Gaia has been pretty kind to humanity over all, although those who have tasted her anger via an earthquake, flood or any other perversions of natural phenomena would hardly agree. However, judged against the human analogy of the usual crop of physical upheavals to which we subject our bodies from time to time (or those resulting from our contact with external chaotic fields such as viruses, etc.), Gaia has, if anything, surely been somewhat lenient with us. After all, much of the natural phenomena which cause us such distress doubtless gives her relief in some form or other, as she must need to move about a bit from time to time to avoid the cramp of physical stagnation.

Chaos science regards the complex nature of all life, which naturally embraces both the upward and downward sweeps of the chaos/order sine wave. Both are essential to the progressive flow of creation at all levels, for without chaos there would be stagnation and without order there would be no form. Surely it is the same with Gaia and her shadow as it is with us and ours: we are ever seeking a state of balance between the two, which is inevitably provided by a third, or 'reconciling force', as depicted in the age-old symbol of the Caduceus.

Over many years I have effected an intense study of the chaos/order sequence, long before such terms became fashionable buzz-words in modern society. Why was it, I asked, that the ancient Egyptians, for example, inevitably chose triads of deities (Neters) to illustrate points in cosmic philosophy? For example, we have the Memphis Triad consisting of Sekhmet, enemy of Chaos, who uses the very forces she despises to carry out her handiwork; her husband Ptah, the Master Builder, whose job it is to effect a more acceptable reconstruction following the chaotic calamity, while their son, Nefer-Tem (beautiful godling), is the Healer (reconciling force or balancer!). The ancient gods of Time were inevitably healer deities, Time itself (which I maintain to be a personalized energy constituting the fifth, or missing component in TOE) being the reconciling factor in the perpetual conflict between chaos and order which constitutes creation.

GAIA - THE EGO

Returning once again to Jung's psychological classifications we are faced with considering the 'I' which is Gaia. In keeping with many ancient beliefs we tend to think of our planet as a 'her' although this was not so in every case. To the ancient Egyptians the Earth was Geb, a masculine entity, and likewise their Lunar Neter, Thoth (Tehuti), Scribe to the Gods and Keeper of the Records of All Time. The latter can be easily answered, however, if one makes a study of past pole shifts, prior to which the Moon did not occupy the same position in our night sky as it does today. Several other ancient peoples also regarded the Sun as feminine, its acquisition of a masculine gender only occurring with the advent of the Silver or Matriarchal age, when the change in the Moon's polarity was doubtless owing to the effect it exerted on the feminine physiology. Gaia herself, being a water deva (water is seen by metaphysicists as a yin or receptive element), would surely qualify as feminine, more so than the Moon which, until recently, anyway (ice having now been detected there), astronauts have assured us is devoid of any surface moisture.

However, if we are to apply the principles of Jungian psychology to Gaia we must accord her both an anima and an animus, which she doubtless has. Perhaps the latter has been mythologized in the deeds of the gods of destruction and reconstruction, so it is not without good reason that Kali is the wife of Siva, who destroys like Time itself but is also merciful (his anima or alter-ego, perhaps, or maybe they are simply two aspects of the same Essence or field?). Either way, the association of Gaia with the deities of Time is undeniable; but then it would be, wouldn't it, since she is a devic essence!

GAIA - THE BRAIN?

Does Gaia have a brain through which she communicates with and modulates her soma? This is something we have yet to discover although there has been considerable speculation among mystics and metaphysicists as to whether such a cerebral network does exist. As hominids, the regulation of our soma is governed by impulses emitted by different parts of the brain in relation to given stimuli which, in turn, may affect the central or

autonomic nervous systems, the mental system or the endocrine
system, each of which also have their subdivisions. Perhaps a
closer look at these systems and how they function in the human
body might serve to give us a clearer impression as to whether
or not Gaia has or, indeed, needs such a complicated array of
'hardware'.

1. *The Central Nervous System*: (CNS). That portion of the
    vertebrate nervous system consisting of the brain and spinal
    cord.

2. *The Autonomic Nervous System*: So named because it acts
    autonomously and consists of two parts, the sympathetic
    and the parasympathetic systems, which assume opposing
    roles in monitoring the internal states of the body. These
    two systems, which are controlled from centres in the
    midbrain beneath the hypothalamus, regulate several bodily
    functions and influence much of the activity of our internal
    organs. Although subject to endocrine and emotional influ-
    ences, they are outside the reach of direct voluntary control.
       The Sympathetic Nervous System operates through two
    chains of ganglia which run one on each side of the
    vertebral column. The incoming nerves to the chain come
    from twelve thoracic segments of the spinal cord. The
    outgoing nerves leave the chain to run in a complex
    network to the heart, lungs, skin, blood vessels and internal
    organs. When stimulated, this system releases adrenaline
    at its nerve endings, a portion of which enters the
    bloodstream to prepare the body for 'fight or flight'.
       Stimulation of the parasympathetic system produces the
    following effects: (a) increases the speed and force of the
    heartbeat and its output of blood; (b) raises the blood
    pressure; (c) constricts some blood vessels and dilates
    others; this results in an increased blood supply to the
    muscles at the cost of a reduced supply to the abdominal
    organs and the skin, thereby redistributing the body's blood
    flow as appropriate for strenuous activity; (d) dilates the
    bronchioles, making for easy access of air to the lungs; (e)
    dilates the pupils of the eyes; (f) causes the skin to become
    cold owing to the reduced blood flow; (g) makes hair stand
    'on end'; (h) activates sweat glands; and (i) tightens up the

bladder and bowel sphincters (although extremes of fear may overrule the latter and cause incontinence).

Sympathetic nervous stimulation is a costly affair in terms of energy and, although well-justified in times of emergency, it is potentially damaging to the body if the system is repeatedly activated in response to emotion that is not allied to physical action. As many of the somatic phenomena of fear are the result of sympathetic nervous activity, the beta-blocking drugs - which selectively block sympathetic nerve action - have become widely used to help protect the heart and blood vessels from over-stimulation, reduce high blood pressure and lessen the effects of nervous apprehension.

3. *The Parasympathetic Nervous System*: This issues from the brain stem and spinal cord in two sections, both of which are controlled from the centre of the midbrain. The nerve fibres of the upper section affect the cranial nerves at the eye, face and head and, most important of all, the vagus nerve. The vagus is the tenth cranial nerve and its old name, the 'pneumogastric' nerve, reminds us of its influence on the lungs, stomach and intestines as well as the heart. The nerves of the lower section run from the lowest segments of the spinal cord to the pelvic organs, particularly the lower bowel, bladder, sphincter and genital organs.

Parasympathetic nerve action produces the exact opposite of sympathetic action, in that it (a) constricts the pupils of the eyes; (b) stimulates salivary gland secretions; (c) slows down the heart, reducing its output and, although it does not directly reduce blood pressure, it achieves this effect indirectly by inhibiting the sympathetic system (and vice versa); and (f) controls contraction in the rectum and bladder by relaxing the sphincters. Sexual activity involves parasympathetic stimulation of the genital organs, although orgasm and ejaculation are the result of sympathetic activity.

The autonomic nervous system, being vulnerable to emotion and immune to reason, is highly susceptible to the kind of external stimuli that can result from psychic activity, altered states of consciousness, astral projection hypnosis, the performance of certain rites, or some of the more pseudo-psychological practices which pass as alternative therapies.

4. *The Mental System*: This system involves those states of mind
   which control the personality, behaviour and feelings rather
   than the physical functions of the human body. These can,
   in turn, affect the physical system, causing what are
   commonly referred to as psychosomatic illnesses.

5. *The Endocrine System*: This consists of the pituitary, adrenals,
   thyroid, parathyroid, ovaries and testes, plus the insulin-
   producing portion of the pancreas. These glands produce
   substances called 'hormones' which are secreted into the
   blood and which act to regulate, integrate and co-ordinate
   a wide variety of chemical processes carried out by the other
   tissues and organs of the body. [3]

But what we now have to ask is, does Gaia, as a self-regulating
entity, exhibit any symptoms which could broadly relate to our
own physical reactions to stimuli from the brain (CNS), the
autonomic system, the mental system and, probably most of
all, the endocrine system? Surely she must have some
mechanism equivalent to our autonomic nervous systems that
would alert her, albeit subconsciously, to possible dangers to
her body, while also ensuring that those physical tasks which
form part of her evolutionary cycle are carried out on a regular
basis (bearing in mind that her time-scale is vastly different from
our own)? So many questions to put to her.

Although Lovelock opines that Gaia is not a 'thinking' entity,
his hypothesis would seem to indicate that she is well aware of
what is taking place on her surface, her reaction being one of
anger. As to her endocrine system: here we enter the realms of
metaphysics since the ductless glands in humans have ever been
related to the chakric concept. Many mystics, in fact, firmly
believe she has chakras similar to our own, although there is little
agreement between the numerous schools of thought on this
subject as to where these are located. Since she has indicated to
me (and others) that she is, in fact, out of balance or positioned
at an angle in relation to the Sun which is far from comfortable
for her, it would seem logical to dismiss any idea of these points
in her body being in a straight line (spine) from north to south
as we know it today. There is a popular metaphysical belief that,
following her next quantum leap, her 'spine' will be straightened
and the chakras therefore positioned correctly for the new input

of higher frequency energies that will come in the wake of her change.

According to Eastern arcane tradition, the chakras are small vortices or force fields, which act as interconnectors between, or transformers for, those energies that pass from the subtle or faster frequencies to the physical body. The number of these manifest in the human physical body is generally believed to be seven, although some nonconformists insist that there are eight or even nine. Original Sanskrit names and other relevant correspondences are shown in the chart as under:

Chakra	Endocrine Gland	Area of the body	Colour
Muladhara	Reproductory organs	Base of spine	Red
Svadisthana	Pancreas	Spleen	Orange
Manipura	Adrenals	Solar plexus	Yellow
Anahata	Thymus	Heart	Green
Visuddhu	Thyroid/Parathyroid	Throat	Blue
Ajna	Pineal	Between the eyes	Indigo
Sahasrara	Pituitary	Top of head	Violet

(Author's Note: There are differing schools of thought regarding the lower three, Mindell, for example, placing the pancreas at the Manipura and the adrenals at the Svadisthana. The above, however, seems to be the most popularly favoured.)

Surely the most interesting of these, as far as Gaia is concerned, are the thymus and pineal glands. The thymus is a ductless gland-like structure situated just behind the top of the breastbone, but unlike the other endocrines it does not act by secreting hormones. Its main role is performed in the latter part of foetal life and in early infancy when it processes lymphocytes, which it endows with the power to distinguish between 'self' and 'non-self' cells and proteins. Processed lymphocytes (*T* lymphocytes) circulate in the lymphatic system and settle in lymphoid tissue (mainly in the lymph nodes). Their successors subsequently alert the body's immune defences against foreign proteins, tissues and micro-organisms, and activate *B* lymphocytes which generate antibodies against foreign proteins and toxins (antigens). Some lymphocytes are

killer cells, a fact which I have always found intriguing since it
appears to indicate that the thymus programmes our future
health from a very early age, being the deciding factor as to
the diseases (killers or otherwise) most likely to afflict us. Could
one not liken these to those computer viruses which, if
undetected, can distort, or even destroy, a whole programe?

The pineal gland is a small, reddish vascular body in the
posterior part of the third ventricle of the brain. Until recently
its function in hominids was uncertain, although in other animal
species it is known to secrete a substance called melatonin which
appears to be connected with skin colour. Recent research,
however, has come to link it with the effect of light and seasonal
variations on the bodily functions. Seasonal depressions are now
believed to have pineal origins. No other part of the brain
contains so much of the neurotransmitter serotonin, or is
capable of making melatonin.

Since science now informs us that we have a genetically
programmed potential for both the plus and minus factors in
life, the supposition that the same principle must also apply to
other life forms should not prove too much of a strain on our
credulity. It is my personal belief (based on years of practical and
metaphysical observation), that the whole evolutionary cycle of
a species is preprogrammed, so the same must surely apply to
Gaia and her kind. Just as the programme carried by our own
thymus predisposes us to certain illnesses, so the 'field' (spirit)
that is Gaia must have taken on her planetary body (particle),
complete with its proneness to specific viruses. And in much the
same way that the human pineal gland responds to light waves
among other things, the probability of Gaia possessing an
equivalent organ that would serve to absorb and reflect energy
emissions from bodies similar to her own, to which she would
naturally react in much the same way as we do to darkness, light,
time, or any of the GUT forces associated with the whole cosmic
creative process, is not beyond the realms of possibility.

Bearing all this in mind it is logical to assume that Gaia does
have a brain of sorts, which computes such information and
passes it to her body, sometimes autonomously but at other
times with full consciousness of what she is about. Where, then,
could such an organ be situated in a spheroid body? In the
ensuing dialogues I intend to ask her.

ENDNOTES:

(1) Cirlot, J. E. *A Dictionary of Symbols*, p.277.
(2) Jung, C.G. *The Archetypes and the Collective Unconscious*,
    Part 1, p.20.
(3) Hope, M. *The Psychology of Ritual*, pp.96-103.

Chapter 4

THE DANUIH EXPERIENCE

This is the point in my narrative at which the particle gives way to the wave and the concept of non-local consciousness begins to intrude into the realm of material rationale although, viewed against the 'New Physics' backdrop, field to field communication, relayed to the brain for decodification, is hardly esoteric! However, anyone setting out to effect a bridge between dialectical materialism and the lunatic fringe is a non starter, so my own stance inclines me towards a central position which acknowledges the validity of unprejudiced scientific research on the one hand and a more left-brain approach to metaphysics on the other. I have little doubt, however, that although my practical application of the field theory is guaranteed to evoke howls of derision from scientific conservatives, it is equally likely to upset those mystics and New Age pundits who are, as the saying goes, 'so heavenly minded that they are no earthly good'.

FIELD CONTACT v. THE CHANNELLING PHENOMENA

Before we go any further, I feel it necessary to draw some positive distinctions between mutual field-access and the current spate of 'channelling', which in my youth used to be referred to as 'trance mediumship'. Some metaphysicists tend to look askance at channelling on the grounds that either the imagination can play too active a part, or that the practice can be conducive to 'possession' or psychic fragmentation. To this must also be added that much of what is served up to us as words of enlightenment, in the form of teachings or promptings from intelligences external to the psyche of the medium, is nothing more than a possible contact with some inner aspects of the channeller's own personal psychological economy. In other words, the audience is being presented with a philosophical or metaphysical summary of any of the following:

(a) The medium's own transpersonal or higher self;

(b) his or her alter-ego;

(c) a suppressed aspect of his/her psyche which has failed to find an outlet for its views in the normal channels of life;

(d) a fragmented section of the mind bordering on the paranoic or schizophrenic;

(e) a convenient way of putting across that which the deliverer would dearly love to express openly but dare not for fear of ridicule - the 'it wasn't me, of course, so don't anyone take offence or ask me any questions about it after' syndrome. (Which reminds me of parapsychologist Dr.Serena Roney-Dougal's definition of channelling as 'a monologue for which nobody wishes to claim responsibility - or to disclaim the power it commands!');

(f) an aspect of the field that has a genuine access to timelessness.

The other problem, of course, lies in the programming already undergone by the channeller. Edgar Cayce is a prime example of this in that his brain inevitably translated information fed to it from the field to comply with the Christian teachings with which he had been indoctrinated in his youth. In ninety-nine per cent of channelling this 'correction' of data supplied is consciously monitored by the left brain in order to accommodate existing schools of belief and therefore remain within acceptable religious codes of the day. This may be evidenced in the inordinate number of channellers claiming exclusive contact with a string of Old and New Testament personalities, Jesus and the Archangel Michael being among the most favoured. The interesting thing (which amuses psychologists no end!) is that these so-called entities frequently contradict themselves when supposedly entrancing their channellers!

THE MECHANICS OF CHANNELLING

As with trance mediumship, most channellers work on the principle of relinquishing their own conscious thinking (left-brain) and allowing the right brain to make contact with the entity. I have, in fact, tried this myself on occasions and the amusing thing about it is that while one's voice is occupied in spouting forth on this or that, one's rational mind can also be co-existing with this event. For example, one can be busy working out the next day's shopping list! Time, also, ceases to exist. One feels one has been nattering on for about ten minutes at the most only to find, upon 'coming round' (assuming left-brain activity consciously), that an hour and a half has passed! A similar phenomenon occurs during sleep state. I recall an old alarm clock I used to have when I was a professional singer working as a member of a major opera company. Some two or three seconds prior to going off it would give a slight click and I would think to myself 'oh, drat!'. But during those seconds I have actually dozed off and experienced a dream sequence which, if enacted in an awake state, would have occupied some three hours at least. Time is, as we know, totally relevant to the frequency in which the experience takes place so that when one is in field contact (the subconscious or whatever according to psychologists) it bears no resemblance to the time decided by those physical factors involving our planet's daily motions, etc.

Some channellers, however, claim that they are not 'taken over', as such, but simply effect a telepathic contact via which they relay the messages given to them. In all of this the subject of error must obviously raise its ugly head, which naturally begs the question: 'How can one tell the genuine from the rubbish?' There is such a practice as 'challenging', or demanding proof of identity, which I have always used. But since this requires some knowledge of the nature of field frequencies while also involving practical procedures, it would be difficult to clarify in a few sentences. Discernment, especially as related to field access, only comes with soul-age (field band-width) and experience, neither of which can be bought or acquired in a few months. Hence the folly of Courses (usually very expensive!) run specially to 'train' channellers.

The ability to negotiate both brain hemispheres with a degree of accuracy, which is what good psychism is all about, is, like the Biblical 'Talent', a gift which needs to be properly handled. Many psychics start out with the best of intentions but sooner or later fall prey to the twin lures of material gain and fame. Added to this is the fact that most people believe what they want to, anyway, and no amount of logic, proof, or whatever, is likely to make the slightest difference as to whether they feel they are being addressed (via a channeller) by some exalted personage from past history, a great religious sage, or bug-eyed E.T. It has often struck me how The Experimenter Effect (see Chapter 1) works so smoothly in cases of the latter. It only takes one writer with a vivid imagination to portray a particular extra-terrestrial he or she claims to have met and from then on almost every contactee describes an identical being or beings!

Applying the field theory to this phenomenon, however, one could suppose that the more genuine channellers have, in fact, touched upon a field of pure energy for which there are no terms of reference in our present world vocabularies, and duly labelled it in the only way they know, be that religious, scientific (oh yes, scientists are just as vulnerable to this although they don't tend to close their eyes and do it in front of audiences), or historical!

A final word of warning - beware the charlatan. A year or so ago I was introduced to a well-known American channeller who boasted openly of his 'wonderful gift'. I questioned him as to who he channelled; the answer sounded like an Old Testament roll-call. 'But surely,' I queried, 'these are all characters from the Bible?' 'You're right on target, honey,' he answered. 'You see, I cover the Bible Belt, and that's where the money is!' And thereupon I rest my case!

FIELD TO FIELD CONTACT

Having said my piece on the channelling issue the question will doubtless arise as to how I actually effect a field contact. Do I close my eyes, make grunting sounds and breathe like a hippo in 'glorious mud'. Heaven forbid! Such behaviour in others embarrasses me to the extent of discomfort and has, I know, put off many would-be believers who fail to see the necessity for theatrical displays. Surely the old shamanic practices of putting on a show to convince their audience of supraphysical presences is unnecessary among thinking people, or am I expecting too much? The fact to be firmly established is that in these dialogues *I am not taken over, nor do I relinquish left-brain consciousness at any time*. For me, talking with Gaia is like holding a conversation with a member of one's own ilk from whom (for some esoteric reason) one has been separated by time and space. On the first occasion she addressed me as 'sister', thus indicating a 'family' connection of which I was already vaguely aware. Nor are all her communications confined to conscious, rational dialogues; she comes to me in sleep state and has accompanied me on many journeys through time, explaining the birth and growth of universes. She has helped me to explore parallel worlds which exist at a similar frequency to our own, and shown me the wormholes which lead to other, more subtle frequencies. Sometimes she just points the way, reminding me of my own knowledge, and I proceed alone. At others, she is with me, especially if the information concerns her immediate welfare and that of her family in this solar system and corner of the galaxy. I think I have always known her.

Instigating a dialogue with Gaia could be likened to keying-in a password on a computer which affords a manifestation of instant entry into the desired program on a Menu. But how can I be sure that this is not simply an aspect of myself as outlined above? Through my communications with Gaia I have been able to recognize, and finally put into place, many of the things I was born knowing. Only one other contact has ever identified itself in this way before - my beloved teacher known affectionately as H.A. (see below). But why now? After all, as I write I am approaching my sixty-fifth birthday. Gaia says, 'You have a term much favoured in your espionage movement - "sleeper". Think about it.'

As with everything else in life there are also dark or chaotic areas in field access. Since this practice is, of course, a two-way thing, one is just as likely to pick up a virus as a genuine connection. As I have explained above, the discernment necessary to overcome this problem does, I assure you, take many, many years to acquire and, since we are all liable to error, never, for a single moment, should one's guard be allowed to drop.

Which brings me to my final statement on the matter: in no way do I make claim to complete accuracy in any of these contacts. I am just as susceptible to imprecision or delusion as anyone else, including Gaia herself, and I know that on occasions neither of us have got it right. So, good reader, make fair allowance; we can only do our best at any one time and, as H.A. has always taught me, intention is the ultimate decider between order and chaos, or what we generally refer to as good and evil, like ever attracting like.

AN ALIEN AMONG YOU

In the light of the above and, in order to explain my life-long lead-up to the ensuing dialogues, I am obliged to bore my readers with the saga of my arrival on this planet on 17th September 1929 and the subsequent events which eventually forced me to face the fact that, although I had entered a hominid body, my field was not primarily of that species. My quest must have been firmly programmed prior to my birth, however, since I was born with full field awareness, the recollection of which I have clearly to this day. For example, I recall as a tiny infant looking down at my new body and thinking, 'I wonder how long it will take me to get this vehicle sufficiently programmed to be of any use?' In another instance when the body was experiencing pain I thought to myself, 'Perhaps this will be its exit door, but somehow I think not.' My non-local component (wave) was well aware of the birth/death process from before I was born, how one came and went, employing each physical vehicle for some specific purpose; my only problem was that this new vehicle and the circumstances surrounding it were unfamiliar to me and therefore needed to be learned about from scratch.

My very strange childhood was punctuated with metaphysical experiences of a similar nature. On one occasion when I was at boarding school I was placed in isolation with two other children who had contacted chickenpox. The Nun who brought us our food called us 'dirty, diseased creatures covered with the marks of the devil' which so incensed me that as soon as she left I shot out of my body, from which vantage point I effected an immediate cure. When she returned later I said, 'See, Sister, I am better, the spots have all gone.' After examining me to ascertain the truth of my statement she crossed herself wildly and backed away muttering to herself, 'She's a child of the Dark One.' A no-win situation, thought I. I was about nine years old at the time.

My first seven years with a wonderful Nanny were not so traumatic, however. (My mother deserted me following my father's demise when I was only three days old.) I never attended school until I became a boarder at the age of eight, prior to which Nanny taught me everything. At six I could read Tolstoy, and any of the daily papers, with ease. That dear soul cued me in as to the ways of the world, the class system, the customs of other nations (as a professional Nanny she had visited and worked in many foreign climes), while also imbuing me with the basics of practical psychology. She was killed in the buzz-bomb raids in WW2. May our fields one day meet and blend.

During my teens when most young girls were thinking of boy-friends, aside from a love of horses and riding I read only medical works and books of a metaphysical nature, so that by the time I entered the Women's Royal Air Force at the age of nineteen I was well versed in such things as astrology, numerology, etc. Medicine was my first love but, having no family to back me, it was not to be.

The next few years I will skip, my only comment being that I soon learned it was not prudent to talk about subjective experiences which were totally alien to most other people I met. In order to get along in society without being labelled a crank or nutter, it paid one to keep quiet. There is a saying: 'In the country of the blind the one-eyed man is king.' Balderdash! In the country of the blind the one-eyed man is a heretic because, sadly, his second eye is, like those of Odin, Horus, and other mythologized Time-Lords, confined to non-locality, thus rendering him/her Cyclopean and partially impotent. To know something instinctively but be unable to find adequate terms of reference via which to express it can lead to much inner frustration. Perhaps some day I'll write an autobiography.

It was not until I was invited to speak at the MENSA Annual Conference at Worcester College in 1993 that I finally decided to emerge publicly from my alien closet. To my amazement no-one batted an eyelid, probably because my approach was via parapsychology and quantum theory rather than mysticism, while at the question-session which followed the whole subject - Time and the Field Theory - was retained at this rational level. As I have already mentioned, circumstances in my youth having denied me the right to a university education, it has taken me a long time to arrive at where I would have been had things been different. Peter Stewart tells me I am a natural scientist and should have entered that profession years ago. But then I would have been denied the varied experiences afforded me by the professions in which I have been engaged - social work/ psychology, music and writing, all of which have helped me to understand both sides of the metaphysical/physical coin.

Throughout my life I have not so much learned from books and lectures as from accessing the databanks of my own field and other non-local sources. People often ask me, 'Who taught you that?' I am obliged to answer, 'No-one, I simply remembered it.' However, although my field-access abilities have always been present, it is only in recent years that I have acquired the terms of reference necessary to expound them publicly - vocally, or in print. The collective programming one receives in one's youth carries a high fear quotient which so often prevents one from speaking out in case one is viewed as weird, spooky, abnormal or, as that ghastly Nun inferred, in the retinue of some infernal power! However, since I do not subscribe to a belief in any such phenomena I can hardly be accused of holding court with it!

I have always had the ability to access other fields, although for a long time I lacked the cerebral programming essential to the decoding and expression of the information received. It is rather like owning a very powerful computer capable of accessing carefully guarded terminals but being unable to effect entry due to disk-program limitations. However, all that has recently changed, I have remembered at least some of the passwords, and my lines back to my own kind are finally opened.

NOT GAIA BUT DANUIH

But enough of me, and now to Gaia. Since my birth I have had a continuous contact with a wonderful being I later came to know simply as H.A. Nor am I the only one to have effected a connection with this multifaceted field, others I know having also experienced it to a greater or lesser degree depending on their

personal and collective programming. In the summer of 1993 I
was approached by a group of people living in the West Country
regarding arranging a meeting of like minds who were aware of
Gaia's impending quantum leap and were consequently anxious
to offer her some small token of help. I suggested a corporate
Rite during which the frequencies could be raised and energies
generated sent lovingly to Gaia. Some days prior to the event,
during a field to field contact with H.A., the suggestion was made
to me that I effect a similar contact with Gaia. My initial reaction
was one of uncertainty. I had never accessed the databanks of a
planetary field before, nor had I allowed such a field access to my
own consciousness; could I do it? The day and hour of the Rite
duly arrived and I found myself at the spot in time allocated to
a possible union of fields with Gaia. It all happened so easily,
rather like meeting up with some blood relative from afar whom
one had heard much mention of but never actually met. In
simple terms, I had finally come home. Since then Gaia has
allowed me access to her databanks and I in turn have made my
meagre knowledge available to her. Much of the remainder of
this book will be taken up with the highly educational and
revealing dialogues which ensued - questions regarding her own
future (and therefore that of mankind and all other species with
whom we share her corpus) and many, many other points of
interest and intrigue on subjects ranging from quantum theory
to the dogmas of world religions.

Oh yes, THE MOST IMPORTANT THING OF ALL: she
does NOT like to be known as Gaia as the name does not accord
with her personal sonic. I asked her if there was another name,
mythological or otherwise, which she might prefer; she chose
Danuih, the old Atlantean name for the Earth Goddess which
later surfaced in the mythologies of the many lands colonized by
The Old Country prior to its sinking. Ladies and gentlemen, I am
much honoured in being able to present to you the Consciousness
(field) which regulates and programmes this planet we call Earth
- the devic Essence, Danuih.

Chapter 5

INTRODUCING DANUIH

In presenting the ensuing dialogues I shall try, where possible, to keep all relevant subject matter together for easy reference purposes although it must be understood that this might not necessarily be the order in which it was received. Some of the questions are my own, others have come from believers and sceptics alike. I may also merge fields with Danuih while actually working on my word processor, something which usually occurs when I am unsure as to her meaning, or she is experiencing difficulty in finding suitable terms of expression in my somewhat limited databanks. Then there are those questions which Danuih has posed to me, to some of which I am able to give a satisfactory answer, others not.

I will endeavour to keep my own comments at a minimum and avoid 'doctoring' her content, although some of the information proferred is guaranteed to give me cause for concern. Scientific substantiation and any other evidence will be effected in ensuing Chapters, wherein I may also occasionally refer to first hand experiences or appropriate anecdotes for exemplification or to demonstrate a point.

I shall simply use 'D' for Danuih and 'M' for Murry. So, here we go!

THE FIELD CONSCIOUSNESS AND NATURE OF DANUIH

M: Danuih, how conscious, or aware, are you as judged against the current human meaning of the term?

D: I am far more conscious than the hominid species overall
    since my consciousness, unlike theirs, is not limited to an
    exalted perspective of my own kind.

M: What exactly is 'your kind', Danuih? Although I am fully
    conversant with your nature and energies, my readers may
    well be unaware of exactly who and what you are.

D: I am a duality, like yourself, in that the intelligence now
    communicating with you consists of a body, albeit spheri-
    cal, and a 'field', which the majority of humankind who have
    been programmed to accept an 'after-life' would refer to
    as a spirit or soul. My body consists mainly of water as has
    already been shown, which must surely indicate that as far
    as my psychology is concerned, like the hominid species, I
    am emotionally orientated and what would be classified as
    'feminine', passive, or yin. Where humankind and I part
    company (aside from the physical shapes we employ
    through which to gather information and thus expand our
    fields) is that I am from an entirely different evolutionary
    stream from them. I commenced my cycle as a water spirit
    - known to metaphysicists as ondines - and, having attained
    to my fourfold nature (absorbed the knowledge and expe-
    rience and qualities of the remaining three elements, air,
    fire and earth), I then 'ascended' (increased my frequen-
    cy) which took me into (again I am limited to your
    semantics, sister, and you to mine for that matter!) the
    realms of the devas, logoi, angels, or whatever you care to
    call them, for such are the planetary genii.

M: And was I right in assuming that you have similar metaphys-
    ical and psychological personal divisions as I defined in an
    earlier chapter?

D: You are quite correct. I do have three 'selves' since you like
    to put it that way, and my chaotic element, or shadow, is
    due to rear its ugly head in the not too distant future. And
    yes, I also have points at which my body makes contact with
    its own field and fields from more subtle dimensions, af-
    ter the fashion of your chakras. There are seven of these,
    but they are NOT at those points popularly supposed by

the majority of metaphysical thinkers. As to the location of either my brain or my chakras, you will have a clearer picture of these after I have (with external help) straightened myself up, so to speak.

M: Could you comment on what are believed to be 'power centres' on your surface?

D: The energies running through my body vary in nature in different places, some being conducive to healing, others to learning, others to creativity and so forth. As for those centres popularly believed to contain powerful energies, do you think for one moment that I would be so stupid as to expose my most vulnerable parts to the profanity of humankind? Since I am fully aware of their propensity for 'taking' rather than giving, I have deliberately blinded them as to where my real power points lie. Let them go on thinking that certain mountains, valleys, wells, etc. are holy places of telluric energy, but rest assured in the knowledge that such believers are totally deluded!

M: Strong words, Danuih. I think I had better change the subject. On behalf of my readers may I ask you if this is your first planet?

D: No, although it is the first time I have had to deal with hominids.

M: Will it be the last?

D: In view of the 'black hole' factor involved in this universe, yes. But I would need to explain a lot to you about other universes before you could grasp the full significance of this remark and I am not ready to so do at this moment in time.

M: You have intimated to me that you are a much older soul or field than many might imagine. I know you are approaching a quantum leap, could you enlarge on this as applied to your personal development?

D: I think you have already said it in your earlier writing. I am

about to enter the final phase in my evolution with this planet. So, too, is the species I refer to as humankind, which
you call 'hominids'.

M: What sort of time-scale are we talking about in relation to
the human factor?

D: Oh, a while yet. Let us say I would equate with someone
approaching their sixtieth year. Use your mathematics to
set your own average life-cycle of between seventy-five and
eighty years against the figures already given for mine in
an earlier chapter, and you will arrive at an approximate
answer which will, no doubt, set some people's minds at
rest for quite a time ahead.

M: Are you in contact with the other planetary genii in this
solar system and, if so, can you access their databanks?

D: Are hominids in contact with *their* families? Perhaps I
shouldn't ask that since so many of them, having lost the
more secure aspects of the tribal connection, have failed
to replace these with a more civilized perspective of group
responsibility and feeling. The answer you want is yes, although we have each undertaken different tasks in our lives.
As with any family, however, we have our 'black sheep' as
you say, although, archetypally speaking, a representative
of chaos is quite acceptable since it teaches us to balance
the chaotic with the orderly. We are also very respectful of
our Mother, the Sun.

M: Why do you refer to the Sun in the feminine? Most astrologers here view it as masculine. And which of the celestial
bodies in your family is the 'black sheep'?

D: The only suns I know that are not feminine are those in
binary or seed systems. The 'masculine' (active, yang, or
whatever) stars go supernova much earlier than their seed
partners. Our chaotic brother is my satellite which you call
the Moon with whom I am for the moment saddled. And
of course he is yang. The hominid females among you
would have a much easier physical passage were their soma

not regulated by the lunar month! But then you have discussed this all with the Crystal People already so there is no need for me to repeat it.

M: And what about 'guides'? There has been much speculation among mystics regarding who or what will overshadow you following your quantum leap.

D: The term 'guides' does not please me. Let me say that different cosmic influences affect my life during varying periods, depending on my needs and their information requirements. The ancient Egyptians and Atlanteans had this right when they taught that there were Neters appropriate to each Age. These Beings are usually from the archetypal universe which is next up in frequency from this one; they in turn are overlooked by others more advanced and so forth. I find it interesting to note how those of humankind who aspire to what they term 'spirituality' inevitably tend to emulate the archetypes, but I will tell you more about that, and which influences will be taking over on my side, when we come to discuss hominid religions in relation to my proposed quantum leap.

M: In the light of your remarks concerning Atlantis, there is bound to be someone who questions your belief in its existence.

D: Let me quash that one to start with. 'Belief' as such does not enter into it. I am fully aware of what has taken place on my surface in the past, thank you very much!

ON COSMOLOGY

M: Coming back to cosmology, as you certainly seem to be well informed on this and related subjects, are you familiar with the antimatter annihilation principle and how would that apply to you as a planet?

D: My knowledge is only proportional to what humankind knows about its own species. The fact that our bodies are larger makes no difference to our acquisition of information about our own kind. Besides, unlike the majority of hominids, we have always enjoyed field access. As for anti-matter, of course I am familiar with its functions. When my body has worn out and no longer provides a classroom for its purpose, my field, like your own, will meet its anti-field and we will thus be elevated to another, more subtle universe. My 'gamma ray' will remain with the dead sphere, however, to be recycled when the visible universe finally collapses.

And yes, I am familiar with both the dark matter in this universe, and other dimensions which also contain what you would term 'antimatter', in that the energies therein could cancel out matter as you know it. Humankind, however, would be advised to confine their definitions of energy to its appropriate compartments, as I am being informed by those wiser than myself that there is some confusion between contacts effected with dimensions of pure energy and those relating essentially to this universe. There is, for example, a universe parallel to this one in which a planet similar to Earth exists, thus allowing all life forms experiencing on my body a variety of options. I am told these may also be multiplied to the extent that the options become infinite, but my only evidence for this lies in my own 'dreams'.

M: Then you, too, dream?

D: If you can label as dreams sensations and experiences beyond those of the physical, yes. Although I do not sleep in the same way as hominids, my consciousness does wander elsewhere to explore other dimensions. I am fully aware that many people have had similar involvements in dream state - places they have never been to, people they have never met, and alternative paths to those taken in their current lives about which they have no knowledge in their 'present'. In truth they are going to find that once their knowledge of both our own and other universes expands, they will be faced with a new perspective, the likes of which could not be accommodated by their broadest stretch of imagination. But for that, of course, they will need to undergo a cerebral mutation and that task lies in my 'hands'!

M: Are you telling me, Danuih, that you are the prime mover in all evolutionary quantum leaps on Earth, these being subject to your personal movements?

D: To a degree, but not entirely, since my own quantum movements are, in turn, orchestrated by the external agencies of a superior energy. Adjustments of my body in relation to the Sun and other planetary influences within this solar system do, however, effect evolutionary trends among all life on my surface. For example, if I cause certain areas to become warmer, to defoliate, or even to become icebound, all living things are obliged to adjust accordingly. As far as this subject-matter is concerned I would like to stop at this point for, although I am fully aware of what is happening to my own body at present, there is much information of a cosmic content concerning faster frequency fields about which I am not sufficiently informed to converse; coupled with the fact that you, sister, have yet to acquire some appropriate terms of reference. Your field actually contains more knowledge on this subject than mine, but there are passwords you still need to remember which are essential to its access.

DANUIH - PLANET OF MUSIC AND HEALING

M: Oh dear, that puts me in my place, so it is back to the scientific drawing board, I fear. But let us return to more immediate considerations: a lot has been talked in metaphysical circles about the true nature of this planet, your body, and what hominids in particular are here to learn. Could you expand on this theme, please.

D: The Time Lord who originally instructed you, whom you refer to as 'H.A.', told you that I am the planet of Music and Healing or, to put it another way, harmony and balance. Therefore, I attract energies which are out of balance, the idea being that, by undergoing a series of field-expansions on my surface, they are able to rebalance sufficiently to move elsewhere in this or other universes. Unfortunately, things have got somewhat out of hand but then they always do when chaos becomes accelerated prior to a quantum leap.

M: Will you comment on the music here?

D: Not yet, since my remarks are guaranteed to give much offence and it is a little early in the proceedings to start 'coming on heavy'; I think that is the term used. After all, I have no wish to put my readers off before we come to the 'juicy' bits!

THE PURPOSE OF OTHER LIFE FORMS ON EARTH

M: Could you tell us about the other life-forms on your surface - how you feel about them. Are they all as conscious as humankind, or yourself for that matter?

D: Some are less conscious than humankind, others more, depending on individuals. Humans are all too apt to judge consciousness, and therefore spiritual evolution or soul age, by the material standards laid down by their own kind. If a species is 'smart' by their standards, meaning it can cope with mathematical equations, build ugly edifices, manufacture weapons of destruction and produce literary works approved of by current standards of critique, then they view it as advanced. Sadly, however, this is far from the truth. The Old Ones created different evolutionary streams to work side by side as a complement to each other, not in competition, each having something to offer which the others lack. For example, aside from looking beautiful, the plant and tree people are there to provide medicines for all species, the domestic animals to be the mental healers and companions of hominids, the wild ones for all to observe in relation to their own progress; and so forth. Every 'field' from the tiniest particle upwards has a purpose. Yes, I call them all 'people', because from my perspective they and humankind are equal species, all of which were designed to be part of what was intended to be a harmonious whole.

M: Tell us more about domestic animals - are some of them very old souls or, in field terms, expanded?

D: When domestic animals with extended fields return to bodies on my surface they are inevitably drawn to circumstances in which they can express their wisdom, according to the nature of their kind. I am aware of the false information supplied by many of your esotericists that all animals belong to some group soul or field, which is utter rubbish. Many have long since individuated from the group in exactly the same way as old human souls. Please remember that the majority - and I mean *majority* - of humankind are still part of the very kind of group entity to which many of them accuse the animals of being permanently attached. And, if they really believe that their fields have previously waded through the mineral, plant and animal kingdoms before arriving at their present exalted (!!!) status, then sooner or later they are in for a big shock. Sadly, the majority of humankind have not yet emerged from the stifling fetters of collective group thinking and instinctive programming; once free from those constricting bonds it will become abundantly clear to you that humanity's belief that it is special is purely an illusion.

M: One question I have been asked to put to you concerns the statement 'nature is red in tooth and claw' which, the questioner feels, contradicts what the Paschats have said concerning animal evolution.

D: Your questioner is quite correct. Nature is red in tooth and claw. What he fails to understand, however, is that his own species is part of that 'nature'. He criticizes the cat for killing a bird or for chasing a mouse, the dog for worrying sheep and the lioness for killing the zebra to feed her young. But do any of these creatures actually *breed* other life forms purely to enjoy the pleasure of shooting them? Humankind does. The fox, hare and deer are not food animals, and yet they are pursued and torn asunder for pleasure. Your abattoirs are red with the blood of cows, pigs and sheep; humankind is, indeed, red in tooth and claw. Mass murderers, in their mutilation of their victims, cause them infinitely more mental and physical suffering than the cat does in the few minutes it teases the mouse prior to the kill. And while those murderers that are *discovered* (rest assured there are many, many more that get away but I see them all!) may seem few and far between, every cat does not torment mice nor every dog worry sheep. The soldier kills his enemy and that is seen as just, yet the cheetah who hunts to feed her kittens is condemned as bestial. Is the animal's instinct for survival less just than that of humankind? Your concept of justice is, I fear, somewhat one sided.

THE NEGOTIABILITY FACTOR

M: Danuih, you are, to all intents and purposes, an alien field. Could you describe this for my readers in terms comprehensible at their frequency?

D: An alien field is any field the frequencies of which are incompatible with those of the observer or observed; in other words, anything which disturbs the rhythm of the observer's field thus causing a chain neuronal reaction.

M: So, the term 'alien' probably means something different to you than it does to us?

D: Precisely. Hominid reactions to minor field disparities are usually fear orientated, mine are not.

M: Are these incompatibilities of which you speak related in any way to the chaos/order sequence and, if so, do they therefore exist at all levels?

D: Incompatibilities exist at all levels in all universes *that I know of at present*, but then my knowledge is limited as is your own. Since people like things explained in human terms I will give them the teaching as my mother gave it to me and as she, in turn, received it from her parents who entered through the time-corridor (I think you call them worm-holes?) in the binary seed star system you know as Sirius. The universe in which we both find ourselves is but one of an infinite number, all of which exist simultaneously *within each other*. However, most of us can only access the fields of those immediate to our own environment, or of a coarser nature (faster frequencies can always penetrate denser ones), unless the field in question has 'descended' to use a popular metaphysical expression. Or, to be more scientific, it could be likened to the photon which can be either a wave or a particle.

M: Descended from where, Danuih?

D: From universes existing in faster frequencies which can interpenetrate imperceptibly the matter of this our own universe. You see, each frequency relates to the mass of an object, so by altering a frequency you actually effect a change in that object's mass. This is how quantum leaps work to effect changes in matter. But to continue my mother's story; the 'space' if you could call it such, which *appears* to separate our universe from the next, is not inhabited in that no-one (field) actually stays there. It is a sort of way-station *en route* to the next level which is occupied by those beings referred to as archetypes. The italics are to emphasize the Observer Effect, everything doubtless appearing different when viewed from another frequency. But then the progeny of Time Lords know more about what lies beyond that than I do, so don't you think the time has come to come clean and enlighten us all?

M: As you well know, Danuih, I have been reluctant to come out of my closet but now that I, like yourself, am in the 'Crone' stage, what people think no longer concerns me.

D: Good. You see, my own knowledge of faster frequency universes is limited; however, I was taught that there was a point at which all time merges into the singular, wherein dwell the Time Lords, those great Beings who manipulate the stuff of which all universes are created because, as you well know, Time is the missing factor in humankind's own assessment of cosmic energy.

THE TIME LORDS

M: Your use of the term 'Time Lords' worries me, Danuih, although you picked it out of my brain, since it has a sci-fi ring about it. Could you please be a little more specific for my readers? For example, why are they 'Lords', and who are their progeny?

D: Time is an impersonal energy. Time Lords are those who understand it, negotiate it and manipulate it for creative purposes. My use of the term 'Lords' is purely arbitrary since there is no gender as such at that level of consciousness. You may add the 'Lady' if it makes you happy, but the problem here surely lies in humankind's inclination to 'transfer' its prevailing gender problems and prejudices onto fields for which such concepts have no meaning. Their 'progeny' are those under direct instruction from them but there is more to it than that. When I come to explain the 'genetic engineering' role played by the Time Lords,* you will see how the appropriate gene is passed to their physical progeny or next in line. A Time Lord's 'apprentices' are always born to him/her since they are destined for the dual role of both student and carrier of the 'divine' gene.

M: In my Paschat times our name for the Time Lords was the Old Ones - do incompatibilities exist among these great Beings?

D: Those beings who have attained to that state are able to balance chaos with order, therefore there is no friction or tension, the energies normally generated by this continual conflict being transmuted into the pure creative energy of Time. Beyond that I know no more. My family taught me that it is always unwise to be dogmatic, as the opening of the next door of consciousness may easily prove one wrong. Dogmas may provide temporary props for limited fields

*See Chapter 9.

(young souls) but sooner or later all are obliged to grow up, even that rather backward race of hominids who use (and misuse) my body.

M: Why can't people here see and understand these things as you and I do?

D: It would not be prudent for me to give you the correct answer to that question and I think you know why. But suffice it to say that the majority of humankind fail to understand that all consciousness does not share the same perspective of life as they do. They tend to translate everything they see, do, or discover in terms of themselves, as though they own the universe. Religion, cosmology (the Anthropic Principle), sociology, everything they touch or conceive of is thus tainted. Their gods and heroes inevitably appear in their own image and likeness bar the few realities that managed to find their way into the more enlightened ancient religions. They appear unable to conceive of the picture from another view mainly because they cannot accept that anything else in the universe enjoys the freedom of consciousness and therefore choice. How very tribal, but, sadly, not in the nicest way! But such attitudes are the inevitable result of a lack of security or cosmic identity.

In earlier times, when humankind lived in small, isolated settlements, exactly the same thing took place, albeit on a lesser scale. The next village down the road became 'the enemy' until, after they had recovered from the 'our totem pole is better than your totem pole' stage, each side eventually came to realize that neither really posed a threat to the other. In time, humankind will come to know its cosmic brethren and in so doing realize the true position they occupy in the cosmic scheme of things. In scanning your databanks, sister (I nearly committed the error of calling you by another name which wouldn't have done at all!), I perceive that there are those who actually believe that their kind alone are gifted with freedom of choice or freewill I regret to inform them that I, too, and all of my kind also enjoy that privilege, so will those who are in error kindly adjust their facts. Thank you.

ON EXTRA-TERRESTRIALS -
HERE AND ELSEWHERE

M: The term 'alien' is also applied in many other ways among
    hominids. For example, immigration departments refer to
    those from other countries as 'aliens'. Also, thanks to
    Hollywood, there is the E.T. syndrome. What do you know
    about extra-terrestrials?

D: They are about, but not in as many numbers as might be
    imagined. Sadly, many reported visitations from beings pur-
    porting to come from here or there in the galaxy are either
    hallucinations or humankind's creative faculties running
    haywire. Sensible people among them realize that there are
    obviously planets somewhere in this vast universe which
    house beings similar to themselves. But there are equally
    other planets upon which vastly different species have
    evolved, some of which you would find very attractive by
    your current standards of beauty and others, perhaps, a lit-
    tle frightening initially. It amuses me to note how few, if
    any, of these 'visitations' involve beings from the latter cat-
    egory who are *not humanoid* in appearance. I must make
    one point quite clear at this juncture; I am not familiar with
    every neck of the cosmic woods and cannot, therefore,
    speak with any authority regarding all extra-terrestrials.

M: Your comment naturally demands that I consider my own
    contact with the Paschats. Is this species, and the Crystal
    People, known to you?

D: Come, come, now. You *know* I know them, and you are also
    aware that their knowledge is greater than my own. But I
    appreciate this question is for the benefit of the readers.
    Neither of these two distinctly different species exists in this
    or the next universe up, after which we come to the regions
    of the formless ones who are pure energy. They only as-
    sume a physical appearance in order to be recognized. After
    all, a bright light or pulsating blob might not appear as cosy
    and cuddly as a furry Paschat, or as stunningly beautiful as
    a silvery-haired Crystal person. For the information of our
    readers, those beings of light who experienced as Crystal

People are concerned at a higher level with the evolution of humankind. The Paschats, however, belong to a group which deals with the balancing of the order/chaos sequence at less exalted frequencies and, as such, are closely overlooked and helped by the Time Lords. Since your initial introduction to the world of personalized physical matter was among the Paschats, the memory of their appearance, lifestyle, etc. is well etched on the databanks of your field. Logical, if you think about it.

M: There is an abundance of literature doing the rounds at present about so-called 'galactic masters', Councils of Nine, and so forth. Any comments?

D: Never heard of them. That is not strictly true, however, since I have picked this information from your databanks. It does not seem to have struck most believers in such phenomena that all of these characters are hominids, similar to humankind. Your knowledge of this material is, I realize, somewhat limited, as I know you tend to give it a miss when it arrives on your doorstep. However, and you can take my word for it, I do not think you would find, for example, a Paschat sitting on such a Council, or a Satyr, or a Centaur, or a Lizard person; or a planetary genius (like myself!) come to that. And yet many creatures from evolutionary streams entirely different from those of humankind have risen to universes of finer frequencies, having ascended without blotting their copybook in the same way as the humankind with which I am saddled.

M: And what about the many, many people around who believe they originated in other star systems, the Pleiades being the most popular?

D: I have made no bones about the fact that humankind are not my own progeny, therefore they must have come from elsewhere in the universe before they landed on my doorstep seeking harmony and balance. My only comment about the Pleiades is, study the Greek myth as the story of the Weeping Sisters is not without foundation; it will give them a hint of the situation there prior to the 'exodus'. From a

cosmic point of view, however, since there is a chaotic element in that constellation (as any of those who have
experienced tears and misfortune following an event which
took place or was inaugurated on 29th degree of Taurus
will well know), caution is advised. Of course there are many
other galaxies which have also spawned hominids, so you
can take your pick.

M: Danuih, you do not seem too comfortable with humankind.

D: Correct. I only agreed to foster them for a period of balancing and now they have become the cuckoos in my nest
in that they eject my own brood and desecrate my body.
Hardly endearing qualities, would you not agree?

M: You are preaching to the converted as you well know. So,
what are you going to do about it?

D: Wait and see. The culling time is nigh, although there are,
of course, those among the dwellers on my body who are
destined to survive to share my golden years with me. So,
I shall obviously make it my business to help retain those
life-forms capable of negotiating my new frequency, be they
animal, vegetable, mineral, or hominid. Perhaps we can discuss this particular subject separately as I know you have a
lot of questions to put to me regarding the physical changes which will take place during my approaching quantum
leap.

M: Thank you, Danuih. I think I'll call a halt to this session and
take a break.

Chapter 6

SUBSTANTIATION AND COMMENTS

ALL IN THE MIND?

In accordance with my usual procedure, I find it appropriate to apply a combination of logic and known facts to any information purportedly coming from sources external to the five normal senses. In the light of our present line of inquiry the first thing to strike me is my own involvement, and the obvious psychological explanations that are likely to be proferred by those adhering strictly to the purely materialistic approach.

Were I in the adjudicating chair I would probably suggest that Danuih was nothing more than an aspect of myself seeking an outlet for protest. However, when viewed objectively, the items protested against are hardly within my province and I am also slightly perplexed by, if not actually at variance with, some of the scientific information given, and Danuih's belligerent attitude towards the hominid species *per se*. My rational mind therefore alerts me to the attendance of two distinct fields, only one of which I am convinced is mine! One could, of course, argue that the communicating intelligence is other than the spirit of the planet Earth and demoniacal associations will doubtless be attributed to poor Danuih by the Fundamentalists. But as H.A. always taught me, intention is inevitably the dividing line between good and evil, or order and chaos as some might prefer, and I certainly do not have it in mind either to deceive our readers, or promote my own ego. As far as I am concerned it is simply a job I have to do before I die, nothing more or less, and I would much rather someone else took it over here and now.

Being the reluctant prophet that I am, when the proposal was first put to me I asked Danuih, 'Why did you choose me?' She replied: 'I didn't, you chose yourself. To use one of your own terms you were a pre-programmed "sleeper" who agreed to act as both a terminal for finer frequency energy and first hand observer for what you call the "Akashic Records", but which I tend to think of more as the Central Computer!' Enough said. I will henceforth shut up and get on with it.

There are, however, certain points in the previous dialogues which do beg analysis. Let us take them one at a time. As a metaphysicist and 'amateur' scientist I am naturally interested in telluric energies and have long suspected that they functioned along the lines Danuih has suggested. However, regarding power centres, she seems to feel that those places popularly accepted as being points of importance on her surface are deliberate misleads. Several locations spring to my mind, Glastonbury and Mount Shasta being two in particular. I have never visited the latter but as far as the former is concerned I could not agree with her more. If there ever was any power there, and I seriously doubt it, it has been desecrated and nullified by the filth to which it has been subjected since the sixties. Pardon me, but those years were anything but hallowed, much as many look back at them lovingly. In fact, to this day we are still cleaning up the sociological and spiritual mess they left behind. I am no Mary Whitehouse and what people do in the privacy of their own homes is their concern. But when their actions begrime Danuih, then that is another matter since I am more of her ilk than I am of humankind, in spite of the body I am obliged to wear for the occasion.

A POLE SHIFT - FACT OR FICTION?

Danuih seems very positive about her quantum leap and that it will generate a pole shift. I intend to ask her more about that after a few of the facts have been highlighted in Chapter 7, Part 2. In recent years, mass tune-ins, sometimes dubbed 'harmonic convergences', have been instituted, during which a concentration of thought-power is sent out ostensibly to help Gaia (Danuih) but also to avert a possible world-scale tragedy. Perhaps the instigators have become aware (either consciously or subconsciously) that some major telluric catastrophe is hovering on the not-too-distant horizon. But how much use will all this be in the light of the fact that Danuih is going to shift her poles anyway, regardless of our meagre protests! Perhaps she wants us to realize that, in the final scene, she is both director and principle actor and we must content ourselves to be part of the lamenting Greek Chorus.

As regards her quantum movements being 'orchestrated by a superior energy', science has this to say - I quote from theoretical physicist Fred Alan Wolf commenting on universal quantum leaps:

> 'If the Universe is in its ground state, then it cannot spill out energy. It cannot quantum leap to a new configuration *unless energy from outside the Universe enters*. However, that energy entering from the outside world would have to be exactly the energy needed to excite the Universe to the first excited state. Any amount of energy flowing in would flow out if it did not have this exact value. Thus a ground state Universe would be stable.' [1]

Exactly the same will apply to Danuih and her quantum leap.

Also relevant to our inquiry is Terry Edwards' mention of *Information and the Internal Structure of the Universe* by Professor Tom Stonier of the University of Bradford which describes how information is a fundamental component of all physical phenomena, whether human or thermodynamic. He tells us:

> 'When a process undergoes a change it is because information has been added to or subtracted from it. Radiation falling on an atom represents, if absorbed, an information input; if the system is reorganized in some way (say an electron raised to a high energy state) then the information content of the atom is increased. Non radiant heat is a process that increases disorder and therefore reduces information (that is entropy increases).' [2]

NUTATION

A scientist friend who is in the know has drawn my attention to certain facts regarding the Earth's nutation which he has described as being akin to the wobble displayed in a spinning top which is gradually slowing down. This being the case, fluctuations in its magnetic and gravitational fields are likely to become increasingly obvious, with effects ranging from escalating deviations in weather conditions and other terrestrial phenomena to an intensification in gravitational pull that could well attract any celestial body that might pass near. But, as Wolf informs us, it will have to be exactly the right foreign body to help Danuih with her eventual flip-over.

According to G. W. C. Kaye and T. H. Laby, in their *Tables of Physical and Chemical Constants*, the inclination of the Earth's equator to the plane of the orbit has been known to vary over long periods, but the actual value at any time is also affected by the nutation in obliquity.[3] Nutation, for those interested, is demonstrated in Euler's angles as illustrated under. Full details and appropriate equations may be checked in the above publication which provides a comprehensive list of the physical constants of the Earth (pp. 18-21), or *The Penguin Dictionary of Physics* (p. 140).

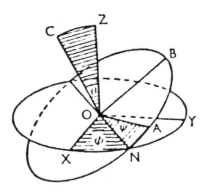

Euler's angles. A set of three angles (θ φ ψ) particulary usefull in describing the position of a body moving about a fixed point O. Cartesian axes, OABC, are fixed in the body (OC usually being an axis of symmetry, e.g. the axis of a top) and yhe motion is described relative to fixed Cartesian axes OXYZ (OX is usually vertical). θ is the angle between the axis of the body OC and the axis OZ. The OAB in the body intersects the plane XOY (usually horizontal) in the *nodal line* ON. The angle $\varphi = \mathrm{X\hat{O}N}$ measures the *precession axis* OZ. $\psi = \mathrm{A\hat{O}N}$ measures the rotation of the body about its own axis OC. Variations in θ are reffered to as *nutation*.

THE WAVERING CONSTANTS

Distinguished biochemist Dr. Rupert Sheldrake has also joined the ranks of those among us who have perceived the subtle alterations taking place around us. In a new book entitled *Seven Experiments That Could Change The World* he comments on recent variations in gravity and the speed of light, for starters. Evidence suggests that when the strength of gravity was measured in the past, results showed a higher energy potential than today, while the speed of light has fallen with every measurement taken between 1928 and 1945. Yet scientists dismiss these discrepancies as incidental on the grounds that their constancy is, to them, an article of faith. Julian Champkin, in his review of Sheldrake's book in *The Daily Mail*, March 17, 1994, comments:

'Something so basic should not be taken on trust. If the fundamentals are changing, then science itself is built on shifting sand. If the interactions between light and gravity change, future ages would have very different physical qualities - and some future time might produce very different sorts of human beings.'

Champkin then goes on to emphasize the error of ignoring The Experimenter Effect (see Chapter 1) under the heading 'Why do Experimenters always find the results they want?':

'A non-scientist might find the obvious answer. Dedicated scientists find even the question shocking.

'Yet in medicine it is known already that the wishes of the experimenter *do* affect what he sees. A researcher tests a new cure on 20 patients and gives a dummy pill to 20 others, to see which group does better.

'But the researcher is never allowed to know which group gets the real pills. Wishful thinking could, subconsciously, affect his decisions. Medical ethics insist on the "double-blind" procedure.

'Physicists, diagnosing the universe, ignore the double-blind protection. They measure only needles on dials, surely things that cannot be affected by wishful thinking?

'But Sheldrake says they can, and evidence seems to be on his side. In experiments where the experimenters are deceived to look for false results - all too often those false results appear. People find what they seek.

'If that applies to ordinary experiments, it would make science really sit up and take notice, or give it a nervous breakdown altogether. The whole of science is based on the supposition that experiments are repeatable, will always give the same answer no matter who does them, or when, or where.

'Can a man's desires really alter the reading on a voltmeter, the position of a needle on a dial? Sheldrake thinks it might be so. The universe he lives in is stranger than we know.'

Bravo Julian Champkin and, of course, Rupert Sheldrake.

Being consumed with curiosity regarding the Sheldrake book I immediately ordered it and have delighted in reading further regarding what the author describes as 'the variability of the "Fundamental Constants"'. Such constants are believed to be changeless and reflect the underlying constancy in nature, and yet detailed investigations have highlighted definite changes over the last few decades. Sheldrake provides the reader with a comprehensive list of these and, although he has far more to say than I would be permitted to include herein, the following comments in particular caught my eye:

'All these constants are expressed in terms of units; for example, the velocity of light is expressed in terms of metres per second. If the units change, so will the constants. And units are man-made, dependent on definitions that may change from time to time ... Old values are replaced by new ones, based on the latest "best values" obtained in laboratories around the world. Below I consider in detail four examples; the gravitational constant (G), the speed of light (c), Planck's constant (h) and also the fine structure constant (α) which is derived from the charge of the electron (e), the velocity of light and Planck's constant.' [5]

Fundamental quantity	Symbol
Velocity of light	c
Elementary charge	e
Mass of the electron	m_e
Mass of the proton	m_p
Avogadro constant	N_A
Planck's constant	h
Universal gravitational constant	G
Boltzmann's constant	k

The Fundamental Constants.[6]

(*Author's Note:* More detailed reading matter on this subject, especially as related to the Earth, is to be found in the Kaye & Laby book mentioned above (see Bibliography).)

Surely the above adds credence not only to Danuih's changing aura but also to the continual fluctuating process of variability or subtle transformation which pervades all life and experience. Much as the corpus of science as a whole refuses to acknowledge that there is anything untoward happening to our world, some of its members do appear to be keeping a wary eye on any foreign bodies in her vicinity that might possibly affect her orbit or alter her present position in relation to the rest of the solar system. The penultimate paragraph in an article which appeared in *The Mail On Sunday* Supplement, *Night and Day* (12th June, 1994), reads:

> 'Speak to any astronomer, and they will tell you that there's a big bang in our future. "For a long time the problem was known only theoretically," says Mark Chapman. "Now we have hard data. Earth is bound to be hit. Statistically, it's certain. The risk of death is higher than in an airplane crash. It's more likely than lots of things people worry about, like botulism, or fireworks, or carcinogens."'

I have a sneaking feeling that when Danuih's 'awaited visitor' does strike, there will be neither the time nor the opportunity to 'nuke' it! As to Champkin's final comment (see above), metaphysicists have ever been aware that, although the principle may be correct, the facts are inevitably coloured by the desire nature.

To return to Danuih. Her reference to her field's eventual meeting with its antiparticle is one thing we can substantiate in science. Every particle, we are told, has an antiparticle, and when one particle collides with its antiparticle both are annihilated, leaving only a discharge of energy in the form of a gamma ray. First you see it, then you don't, sort of thing. Of course nothing in this or any other universe is ever completely annihilated, recycled, maybe, but not finished for good! So, where does it go? Into another universe, of course, wherein it assumes mass of a different density so as to be imperceivable or immeasurable by our present instrumentation. In my book, *Time: The Ultimate Energy*, I have referred to the emitted gamma ray as a signature in the register of the school we call life in this universe. 'I have been here, I have learned here, and this is me finally signing out' sort of thing.

GENETIC MUTATIONS

Cerebral mutations; a subject guaranteed to interest me immensely since the Crystal People touched on it lightly in their communications two years ago. Changes in frequency would, it seems, cause genetic mutations since there would be a degree of radiation emitted as a result. Those who would like to know how this works are referred to *The Paschats and the Crystal People*, Chapter 4. However, to be brief, the role played by radioactivity in evolutionary quantum leaps is important, in that a high increase precipitates genetic mutation in DNA which then becomes the deciding factor as to the quality and frequency of the ensouling field. Denser or slower fields which are incapable of negotiating the new physical waveband are thus automatically barred from entering, resulting in an overall rise in the evolutionary level of the race or genus in question. So, where does Danuih come into all this?

The popular television science series *Horizon* (BBC 2, 8 p.m., March 1994) featured the work of American fossil expert Dr.

Dean Falk, and Liverpool physiologist Peter Wheeler, who had been researching further into the 'Lucy' mystery (see Chapter 2). Challenging the theory that Lucy and her kind evolved into humans because their bigger brains required them to walk upright and thus adjust their knee joints, Falk hit upon the idea that standing tall was somehow linked with *changes on the Earth's surface connected with heat distribution* which required the beings in question to 'walk tall' in order to keep the brain cool. Wheeler substantiated this theory with experimentation, while it was subsequently discovered that, following the Lucy episode in our history, cavities developed in the brain allowing the blood to circulate in a cooling fashion. Thank you, Danuih.

THE PLEIADIAN MYTH

The question of contacts with extra-terrestrial sources inevitably rears its dubious head and I for one am happy to accept the suggestion that delusion is ever hovering in the background. Danuih's reference to the Pleiadian myth of the Weeping Sisters does seem to beg scrutiny, however, so let us see what we can come up with. My encyclopedia defines the Pleiades as: 'An open star cluster in the constellation of Taurus, consisting of several hundred stars, of which six or seven are visible to the naked eye. Also called the "Seven Sisters".'[7] One must therefore assume that it is the six or seven visible stars that are at issue here. Since Danuih has signified that the myth (of which there are several versions) carries either some historical cosmic import, or esoteric significance, it might pay us to examine it:

> 'The Pleiades were the daughters of Atlas and Pleione or Aethra. There were seven of them: Maia, Taygete, Electra, Alcyone, Celoeno, Sterope and Merope. The first three were loved by Zeus, Maia becoming the mother of his son, Hermes; Poseidon won the favours of Alcyone and Celoeno, while Sterope became Ares lover. Poor old Merope, however, was landed with a mere mortal, the cunning liar Sisyphus, as a result of which she shines less brightly in the sky than her sisters. However, prior to their celestial installation they were pursued across the mountains of Boeotia by the hunter, Orion, and were about to fall into

his clutches when their cries for help were heard by Zeus, who turned them into doves and placed them in the sky for safety. Another version of the tale tells how the Pleiades became inconsolable on the death of their sisters, the Hyades, and killed themselves in their grief. Zeus, being moved to pity by their tears, changed them into stars. Their appearance in the sky in mid May usually heralded good weather whereas the appearance of the Hyades was the signal for the rainy season, their name actually meaning "Rainy Ones". According to Robert Graves, however, Merope deserted her six starry sisters in the sky because she was married to a mortal, and a criminal at that, and has *never been seen since.*'

Does that not tell us something? I, for one, certainly get the message!

No doubt those who believe themselves to have Pleiadian origins have fully investigated this myth and appropriated themselves a planet in one of those star-systems accordingly. However, as one who has personally suffered from the results of a venture inaugurated on 29th degree of Taurus, I am jolly glad I am not from that neck of the universal woods!

THE ARCHETYPES

Danuih's reference to the realm of the archetypes is, of course, of great interest to the Jungian psychologist. My own work, *Olympus: Self-Discovery and the Greek Archetypes*, deals with this theme in some detail. Many psychologists seem to prefer the Greek archetypal forms to those of other pantheons, probably because of the precision, clarity and logic of Greek thinking as evidenced in the Classics. Personally, I have also found much of interest in the Neters of Egypt although, unlike the Greek and Sumerian tales, these tend to carry scientific connotations rather than aspects of hominid psychology. For those of my readers unfamiliar with the term 'archetype', Carl Gustav Jung has defined it as:

'A primordial image or idea ... The inborn mode of *acting* has long been known as *instinct*, and for the inborn mode of psychic apprehension I have proposed the term *archetype*. I may assume that what is understood by the instinct is familiar to everyone. It is another matter with the archetype. What I understand by it is identical with the "primordial image", a term borrowed from Jacob Berckhardt, and I describe it as such in the Definitions that conclude this book. I must here refer the reader to the definition "Image".

'The archetype is a symbolic formula which always begins to function when there are no conscious ideas present, or when conscious ideas are inhibited for internal or external reasons. The contents of the collective unconscious are represented in consciousness in the form of pronounced preferences and definite ways of looking at things. These subjective tendencies and views are generally regarded by the individual as being determined by the object - incorrectly, since they have their source in the unconscious structure of the psyche and are merely released by the effect of the object. They are stronger than the object's influence, their psychic value is higher, so that they superimpose themselves on all impressions.' [8]

This concept suggests that the aspect of our psychological economy which connects us with the collective unconscious also alerts us, again albeit subconsciously, to the influences which emanate from the universe of the archetypes to which Danuih has drawn our attention. Since these archetypes appear to be fairly constant in relation to the hominid experience, we all tend to enact their roles to a greater or lesser degree, including their shadowy sides. For example, we are all familiar with the typical or archetypal father; likewise the maternal figure which repeats itself in the pantheons of every nation. Solar deities and Sacrificial Saviour figures are yet two more archetypal figures I have discussed with Danuih at some length, the details of which will be appearing in the chapter on Religion. Danuih appears to be thoroughly cognizant of the main archetypes dominant on her planet, while she herself has been labelled by mythologists as 'The Earth Mother'. Sorry, but having come to know her I am not entirely in agreement with this assessment. In fact, I cannot help feeling that, were she to incarnate among us, she would end up as a jolly good doctor, a highly gifted musician/singer or, more likely, a competent psychiatrist.

THE SOLAR MOTHER

The next issue from Danuih's copious information which demands consideration is her reference to the Sun as her mother. How much do we really know about the formation of this solar system? Did the Sun actually spawn the planets or is there another explanation? Let us see what science has to tell us; here is the version given by my Illustrated Dictionary: [9]

THE FAMILY OF THE SUN
A few large objects and thousands of small ones from patterns that suggest their origins

The Solar System consists of the Sun itself, nine planets, almost four dozen satellites, thousands of small, rocky asteroids, and an uncounted number of comets. The Sun makes up some 99.9 per cent of the Solar System's mass, and most of the remaining 0.1 per cent is taken up by the giant planet Jupiter.

The planets fall into two groups. The terrestrial planets are small, dense, and close to the Sun. They are separated by a belt of asteroids from the giant planets, which have gaseous surfaces and relatively small solid cores, most of their globes being liquid. The exception is Pluto, a frozen world with an orbit so eccentric that it is sometimes nearer the Sun than Neptune (as now, for a 20 year period 1979-99).

The planets, revolving in elliptical orbits that are nearly circular, are held to the Sun by gravity. The closer they are to the Sun, the faster they must move to counteract the Sun's greater pull. Mercury travels round the Sun in 88 days, moving at 48 kilometres (30 miles) a second. Pluto's year is 248 Earth years and it moves at three miles a second.

THE SOLAR SYSTEM

A FLAT, ORDERED SYSTEM *Taken as a whole, the Solar System's most noticeable feature is its flatness. All planets are in the same plane. Moreover, all orbit in the same direction. This suggests that the solar family condensed out of a revolving cloud of gas and dust. Several aggregations of matter came together, the biggest of them being the Sun.*

The Sun would have driven off the lighter-weight materials, including hydrogen and helium, from the inner planets - hence their density compared with the gaseous outer ones. This theory also suggests the notion that planetary formation would be a common result of the formation of any star.

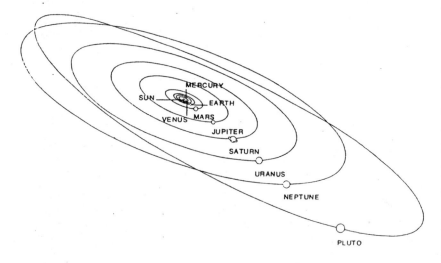

From the above it would seem that we are dealing not so much with a 'birth' situation as that of an organizing intelligence behind the solar system which, if we are to take Danuih's word for it, is what is referred to in metaphysics as the Solar Logos. Her insistence on its passive (feminine) nature is nothing new, however. Many ancient civilisations worshipped the Sun as a goddess. There were sun-goddesses in the lands of Canaan, Anatolia, Australia, Arabia, among the Teutonic and Scandinavian peoples, the Eskimos, Japanese and Khasis of India, to take but a few examples, several of these later acquiring subordinate lunar brothers. Lunar dominance, especially in the feminine form, did not appear to surface until the Silver Age defined by Hesiod, which undoubtedly equates with the matriarchal period associated with the Zodiacal Age of Cancer (c. 8000 - 6000 B.C.).

I have, in fact, investigated the question of Sun/Moon/Earth polarities in an earlier work, *Essential Woman*, in which I wrote:

> 'If Gaia and her satellite are so closely linked, perhaps the polarities have become confused over the ages, after all, as any astrologer will avow, the moon *reflects* in much the same way as a mirror. Is it therefore, like Dorian Gray's famous picture, reflecting some imbalance in Gaia or her progeny? Or is it, perhaps, the lunar polarities that have deviated and "she" is now "he" or vice versa as the stories of Thoth and Sîn might connote.'[10]

I know Danuih will rebuke me by saying, 'Told you so, you knew it all the time,' but there are still aspects about which I would like more information from her; the Crystal People's story of the cosmic virus, for example. No, Danuih, I regret to say I shall have to ask you to tell all. But please accept this by way of a humble request rather than a demand as I know that, in accessing my databanks, you will do anyway.

There is, of course, much more I would like to add regarding Danuih's information and method of approach. For example, she knows I am uncomfortable about her reference to Time Lords among other things, although I am quite aware of her meaning. Besides, were I to change the presentation of her message to bring it in line with that which is more acceptable to orthodoxy (avoiding what is often viewed by psychologists as the hysterical side of metaphysics), I would be just as guilty as those unscrupulous persons past and present who deliberately tamper with the teachings of the sages in the cause of religion, politics or personal power. Since I am in none of these camps I think I'll pass and leave it in Danuih's capable 'field'!

ENDNOTES:

(1) Wolf, F.A.*Parallel Universes*, p.195.
(2) Edwards, T. *Quantum Domains, Chaos & The Theory of Fractogenesis*, p.7.
(3) Kaye, G.W.C. & Laby, K. *Tables of Physical and Chemical Constants*, 2nd Ed. Longmans, 1959, p.21.
(4) *The Penguin Dictionary of Physics*, p.140.
(5) Sheldrake, R. *Seven Experiments that could change the world*, p.p. 164-165.
(6) *Ibid*, p.165.
(7) *Reader's Digest Great Illustrated Dictionary*, Vol. 2, p.1306.
(8) *Dictionary of Analytical Psychology*, C.G. Jung, pp. 47, 48 & 84.
(9) *Reader's Digest Great Illustrated Dictionary*, Vol.2, p. 1589.
(10) Hope, M. *Essential Woman*, pp.23-24.

PART 2

DANUIH - THE FUTURE

Chapter 7

THE POLE SHIFT PHENOMENON

Earlier discussions with Danuih would seem to indicate that she intends to alter her axial position in some way or other regardless of our meagre protests, but how, and when, still remains a mystery. Will she or will she not be more forthcoming? Only time will tell but, rest assured, I shall do my level best to find out as much as I can before the conclusion of this book.

END OF MILLENNIUM HYSTERIA

Irritating as it may be to the more rational among us the escalation of chaos world wide does look set to coincide with the closing years of the twentieth century and early days of the twenty-first. Now the end of any millennium is guaranteed to evoke a barrage of hysterical prophetic utterances, usually from such obvious channels as extremist metaphysical groups, fundamentalist religious cults, and that somewhat questionable phenomenon labelled 'the lunatic fringe', which conveniently encompasses anyone who has managed to escape from the stereotyped programming of the major collectives. But, aside from the odd sensationalist article in the tabloids and, since it would not appear to exert any noticeable effect on the tenor of their lives, most of this material has, in the past, tended to pass unobserved over the heads of the majority.

This time round, however, we are faced with a rather different situation. The PODS (prophets of doom) have received more than a modicum of backing from the barrage of scientific reports of volcanoes and earthquakes causing the Earth to move and similar terrestrial and extra-terrestrial phenomena now being observed, plus the body of everyday physical evidence available for all to view. For example, weather conditions world wide have gone haywire (snow in mid summer in New South Wales; heavy rain and hail in Saudi Arabia; tropical climate in Thailand suddenly turning to freezing - I have a file packed with similarly disturbing data from across the globe!). Add to this the feeling of impending calamity that is permeating all walks of life, which doubtless originates from the hominid collective unconscious, and the flames of the fire of imminent disaster are receiving more than their quota of fanning!

A decade or so ago even a hint of some world-wide calamity would have been politely dismissed as sensational rubbish, but not so today. Warnings of a possible Greenhouse Effect, backed by fluctuations in global weather conditions, have spawned a battery of speculations as to what lies ahead for this planet, which have served to generate a prevailing air of unease. Consequently, many people are experiencing a feeling of inner panic which is neither allied to over-rapid technological changes, or simply things being different from what they used to be. Localized cataclysms and natural disasters in isolated spots on the globe have always been around, while many of us have experienced the throes and woes of major international conflicts. What we are dealing with now, however, is of a subtle and radically different nature, and it is *world wide*.

I was first alerted to the possibility of a pole shift or axis tilt as far back as the nineteen-fifties. At the time it seemed all too vague and far away to have any real impact on those of us who were confronted with its possibility. But as time progressed the evidence started to roll in; slowly at first, but with increasing acceleration of late. My collection of data therefore goes back almost forty years, and my publisher, for one, feels that the time has come for me to present it for acceptance or rejection, as the case may be; unless, of course, the process of publication and distribution is punctuated by lead-in events of the kind calculated to leave no doubt in the minds of my readers. Maybe Danuih, in her wisdom, may even see fit not to pre-empt my warnings. Either way, she does assure us that she will give ample and very obvious foretokens to those who have the sensitivity to heed them.

Before embarking on the terrors of the ensuing chapters, however, there is one thing I must make quite clear; I make no claim whatsoever to being favoured by 'higher powers' with exclusive knowledge of future events, nor am I suggesting that my own conclusions merit the accuracy tab any more than the next person's. It will therefore be up to the reader to take the evidence presented and draw his or her own conclusions unless, of course, Danuih herself decides to step in and settle the matter!

WHAT IS A POLE SHIFT/AXIS TILT?

Since early in this century, disaster movies and novels have served to line the coffers of many a publisher and film company, the ever-expanding popularity of the cataclysmic theme obviously affording people worldwide some kind of voyeurish thrill. Most popular of all are those stories connected with outer space, aliens and the apocalyptic scenario which, in 1979, evoked from *Time* magazine a roundup article entitled 'The Deluge of Disastermania'. Needless to say, certain fundamentalist religious groups have made hay with the latter, while the nuclear fears of the cold-war years also served to add fuel to the idea of some universal destruction engineered by an angry deity.

Although the threat of global war still hovers menacingly in the background, the nuclear bogey has, of late, taken a back seat, its destructive potential paling in the light of an even greater threat to *all* life on Earth - the possibility of a pole shift, or axis tilt. The term 'pole shift' implies a movement of the North and South poles caused by a radical displacement of our planet's axis of rotation. In other words, an event in which, according to some sources, the shift could be as much as 180 degrees.

Possible causes for this vary, there being more than a few alternatives from which to choose. For example, our planet could be knocked out of its present orbit by some passing cosmic body, thus changing its angular position in relation to the Sun, suffer a slippage of its solid crust over its molten interior causing alteration in the polar locations, or experience a sudden build-up of heat (the Greenhouse Effect) which would melt the solar ice-caps, resulting in a possible redistribution of ocean waters worldwide. In fact, theorists toying with 'ultimate disaster' are faced with a sea of possibilities. For example, in his book, *Pole Shift*, John White offers us the following list:

NATURAL
I.   ASTROPHYSICAL
     A. Planetary alignment.
     B. Minor orbit of the earth.
     C. Unusual sun-moon relation.
     D. Passing celestial body (comet, dark star, planet).
     E. Impact by a celestial body (meteorite, planet, comet).
     F. Magnetic or gravitational null zones.
     G. Change in solar radiation.

II. GEOPHYSICAL/CLIMATOLOGICAL
     A. Polar ice-caps increase and/or decrease.
     B. Change in surface mass loading (due to erosion, mountain
         building, coastline changes, isostatic rebound, reduced
         water tables, glaciation, etc.).
     C. Magnetic field disappears or reverses polarity.
     D. Convection currents in the core and/or mantle.
     E. Earthquakes and volcanic eruptions.

HUMAN
III. SOCIOECONOMIC
     A. Atmospheric pollution and greenhouse effect.
     B. Mining, drilling and damming.
     C. Nuclear war and nuclear testing.

BIORELATIVE
     A. Thought forms.
     B. Etherian physics and orgone weather engineering.
     C. Psychotronic weapons.
     D. Intervention by higher life forms.[1]

A somewhat daunting list, which the author has followed up
with appropriate scientific observations. From what I gather,
though, White has altered his views somewhat regarding pole
shifts since the last print of his book in 1988 and, after perus-
ing some of the other data he has produced therein, I think I
know why.

     However, a genuine clue has, perhaps, already been given to
us by Lovelock in his famous prognosticative television interview
in which he spoke of the age and evolution of Gaia (Danuih),
dwelling at some length on the various life-forms that go to

regulate her body. Among the information he proffered to his viewers concerning her nature and future was the statement 'any species noxious to those around it will be destroyed, or destroy itself', which struck me as being highly significant. Humanity, he believes, has broken the rules and has so far managed to get away with it, but if we continue to prove destructive to Gaia (Danuih) we are expendable, as she will resist any changes that do not accord with her own evolutionary pattern. Algae and trees, for example, help her to regulate her body and keep in good health and, although she may have experienced the odd assault from outer space in distant times, a blow from a small extraterrestrial body such as a planetesimal would not kill her.

We have already discussed how many adherents to Lovelock's famous Hypothesis have taken his premise a stage or so further by ascribing to Gaia (or Danuih, as she prefers to be called) a depth of intelligence, consciousness and awareness that is not only cognitive of the changes taking place on her surface, but also responsible for their orchestration. Over vast periods of time she has provided rich soil for the growth and experience of many different life-forms, from organized group entities to individuated fields of consciousness encompassing varying levels of awareness. According to the evolutionists, microorganisms and bacteria formed the basis of life as we recognize it and, as such, effected the groundwork essential to the future growth of the elements of which our bodies ultimately came to be formed. We still host many of these bacteria and rely on them for a balanced state of health.

During her growth process, it is only natural for Danuih to adjust her body in order to accommodate changing modes in both her physical and transpersonal development. Such movements may cause variations in the positions of the poles resulting in the rise and fall of lands, change of climates and shifting of oceans. In much the same way, a wise and ecologically conscious farmer will plant wheat one year and cabbages the next, followed by a fallow period to enable the soil to replenish its nutrients and effect a natural balance. Lovelock commented on how we, in our selfishness, see everything in terms of our own wants or conveniences, whereas Danuih tends to view the events taking place on her body in more holistic terms. It is not the plants, trees, animals, bacteria or algae that contaminate her surface, says Lovelock, it is *people*.

So, are we any the less expendable than the dinosaurs? Have we, in fact, already served our purpose here, which heightens our expendability factor? Lovelock also referred to a 'dark' side of Gaia, her shadow (see Chapter 3), which is well represented in mythology, retribution inevitably being dispensed by avenging goddesses who were nothing if not ruthless in their punishment of the transgressors. When writing my book, *Time: The Ultimate Energy*, I drew my reader's attention to the fact that the goddesses of destruction and regeneration were inextricably bound up with the gods of Time, while both groups of deities could be seen to represent sound scientific principles which form part of the pattern of knowledge readily accepted in many areas of science today.

If, as Dr. Lyall Watson has suggested, time does exist in stationary bands through which we pass, then surely evolution generally, and that of Danuih in particular since this is germane to our present subject matter, is also closely linked to the *tempus* factor, or band of time through which our planet is at present passing.

THE QUANTUM LEAP FACTOR

In physics, a quamtum leap or jump is defined as the transition of an atomic or molecular system from one discrete energy level to another. It usually occurs with absorption of emission of radiation having energy equal to the difference between the two levels. In common parlance, however, the term is often applied to any abrupt change or step from one level or category to a quite different one, especially in knowledge or information.

Assuming that Danuih as an evolving body follows the regular pattern of quantum leaps observed in minute particles, could it be that with each quantum leap, or evolutionary forward-thrust, she is removed to a different time band or frequency, resulting in a new direction for all those life-forms to whom she gives succour? This would account for the removal of the dinosaurs and other species which, from time to time, she finds unsympathetic to, or uncooperative with, her growth process. We may work tirelessly to preserve certain species, but what if Danuih wishes to dispense with them, or us for that matter?

The metaphysical answer is that frequency changes around a

planet involving both the subtle levels which our present technology may suspect but cannot yet prove, and those acknowledged forces that scientists are at present striving to unite into a G.U.T. or T.O.E. (Great Unified Theory or Theory Of Everything) will also undergo radical changes, should Danuih elect to rearrange her physical structure. As has already been discussed, faster or finer fields can interpenetrate lower frequencies but not the reverse. So were Danuih to move into a new frequency band (extend her personal field band-width to include faster energies carrying a more highly radioactive charge), only those life forms capable of accommodating the change would survive. I shall, however, be dealing with the survival factor in a later chapter.

BOHM'S THEORY AND COMPLEXITY

In Chapter 2, I drew the reader's attention to Professor David Bohm's exploration of the notion of the universe as a 'top down' conceptually based environment, implicate being non-dimensional as against explicate which is dimensional. Terry Edwards, who has undoubtedly espoused Bohm's work fully (see Chapter 1), adds the following comment: ' "You" are not your atoms but a being that employs cells and molecules to express the fundamental concept that is "you".' [2]

What both Bohm and Edwards are trying to emphasize, however, is that all life forms are both intertwined with and interdependent on each other, which dismisses once and for all the myth of the supremacy of mankind. This interweaving thread between the quantum worlds and the hominid condition is beautifully illustrated by Roger Lewin in his book, *Complexity: Life on the edge of chaos*. Lewin, a science writer of considerable renown, introduces his 'Acknowledgements' with the sentence: 'The science of complexity turned out to be one of the most intellectually stimulating sets of ideas I've come across for a very long time ...' Lewin then proceeds to enlighten his readers regarding the folly of the reductionist approach. All good stuff in support of Danuih!

Levels of organization from molecules to the central nervous system [3]

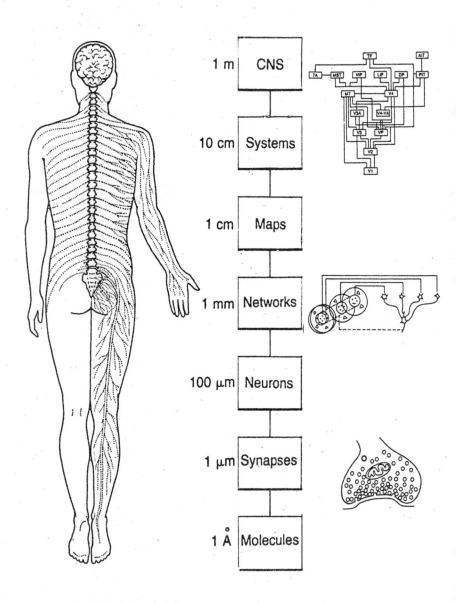

THE CHAOS/ORDER SEQUENCE

The ongoing, alternating sequence of chaos and order is well acknowledged in many disciplines, the time factor, among other issues, being decided by the length, amplitude and phase of the wave involved. As history bears witness, periods of order are inevitably followed by periods of chaos. However, just as the highly structured rigidity imposed by long spells of order inevitably succumbs to entropy, chaos is likewise inexorably accentuated prior to a return to the former. We do not need a prophet or seer to tell us that about the escalation of chaos world wide; it is obvious for all to observe, regardless of their religious or ideological beliefs. Much as we might choose to bury our heads in the sand the inevitable will be, and the portents are now clamouring angrily for recognition and acknowledgement.

A NATURAL PHENOMENON

In the light of the aforegoing, pole shifts are nothing more or less than natural phenomena, a series of growth experiences through which a planet passes in much the same way as we move from childhood to puberty, thence to adulthood and finally to old age. And, as an infinitesimal part of Danuih's implicate/explicate order, we are of no more or less importance to her than the fruit-fly, the lion, or the minerals that are embedded in her crust. Bearing all this in mind why are we lumbered with myths concerning the wrath of the gods, divine justice, Nemesis, etc.; and does the fact that we are the perpetrators of evil deeds (chaos inducing acts) mean that we are in some way influencing Danuih negatively, or interfering with her natural evolutionary cycle? We are neither that clever nor that powerful, although there is a school of thought which subscribes to the theory that the evils perpetrated against her by mankind will serve to accentuate the severity of her transition (or transmutation) to her latter years.

The earlier mentioned description of consciousness as a field of active particles begging organization comes to mind as relative to Danuih's prospective quantum leap; perhaps she is on the point of organizing her chaos and, if we fail to follow suit, there will no longer be room for us on her spring-cleaned surface. But take heart for, when that chaos once again gives way to order, the promise of a much prophesied Golden Age could become a reality!

DANUIH'S POLE SHIFT, AND RELIGION

The totally erroneous and misleading myth of the supremacy of mankind over all else on Danuih's surface must be placed fairly and squarely at the portals of those major religions which perpetrate this cosmic heresy. If we give our planet credit for being an intelligent entity in her own right, whose bosom has nurtured many, many life-forms before the advent of hominids, much as their leaders may protest as to the supraphysical origins of their doctrines, logic demands the view that she is not influenced by the tenets of any of the man-made religions. After all, the minute organisms that live on our bodies do not automatically adopt our beliefs; in fact, they frequently rebel against the conditions imposed upon them by those faiths, as many psychologists or psychiatrists will confirm. It has often struck me that they probably view our brains as their deities, any assault against their natural functionings being taken as the machinations of some evil entity! Anyway, as Danuih herself will be having a lot to say about hominid religious beliefs in a later chapter it would be audacious of me to attempt to pre-empt her. I could well be wrong!

Endeavouring to interfere with Danuih's Rite of Passage in order to save either our own skins or our present order of society could be seen as tantamount to forbidding a teenager to mature or an older woman to enter the menopause! As Danuih has already told us, when she moves it will be via a combination of her own motivation plus an injection of the exact external energy required to effect a quantum leap, and not at the instigation or command of some deity currently espoused by popularly favoured hominid religions. This does not mean, of course, that she is not in tune with finer dimensions; the very nature of Bohm's Implicate Order suggests that she is and it is we who are out of sync, both with her and the cosmos generally. The fact is that Danuih is due for an evolutionary quantum leap anyway, and the sooner we can accept this as a natural phenomenon rather than the wrath of Zeus, Jehovah, Siva, Allah, or whoever, the sooner we will re-establish our natural links with both Danuih and our own cosmic roots and, in so doing, come to understand what she wants of us.

Perhaps we will be among those destined to live through the pole shift: was it not Plato who commented that every catastrophe has its survivors, while also observing sadly how 'the stream from heaven descends like a pestilence, and leaves only those of you who are destitute of letters and education: and thus you have to begin all over again as children, and know nothing of what happened in ancient times'. [4]

THE OVERALL PICTURE

What would actually happen if the poles shifted radically? Would it be the 'end of the world'? Are we dealing here with some 'ultimate disaster'? Hardly. But the going would be pretty horrendous for everyone, although it would obviously be worse for some than for others, depending on where one is in relation to the changes. Let us consider a few of the more obvious manifestations of a pole shift: enormous tidal waves would sweep across the globe as the oceans were displaced by the changing gravitational forces; electrical storms carrying winds of unimaginable speed would raze all but the strongest buildings to the ground; earthquakes would shake the foundations of cities and countryside alike, and in places where they have never before been experienced; the Earth would likewise erupt causing huge lava flows and releasing poisonous fumes which would hang over the ash-ridden atmosphere like a pall. Add to this the loss of public utilities as sewers are broken, gas mains fractured and electricity supplies cut off and, depending of course on which part of the newly oriented globe you find yourself, you could either cook or freeze!

The climate where you are living could, of course, change overnight, just as the new geographical contours of the world would be unrecognizable were you to view them from a space satellite. Remember how the Siberian mammoths were frozen suddenly while partaking of a repast of buttercups and fresh, green grass *of the kind found in temperate climates*? Yes, it could be as quick as that. The heavy ice that now occupies the polar regions could be moved to the Indian sub-continent, or central Africa, while Antarctica and the northern territories could find themselves in the tropics. Of course, many organisms would be totally destroyed, including people. But it will be Danuih who, via her new frequency, effects the choice as to whom and which she wishes to stay as her guests and humankind, for all its supposed supremacy, will have no say in the matter whatsoever. In fact, flora and fauna and insect life have already started to make their appropriate moves, with tropical and subtropical species beginning to appear in what are now temperate climes. Pharaoh ants, click beetles and scorpions, for example, are proliferating in the south of England!

Many of the land masses we now see on our atlasses will no longer be there, but resting peacefully beneath the newly formed ocean basins. Likewise, new lands, that Danuih in her wisdom has left fallow to recuperate beneath her icy wastes or within her Poseidonian depths, will once again show their faces to the Sun, but from which direction will our solar star then be rising? Certainly not the East, of that we can be sure. But more of such speculation later; after all, Danuih herself might deign to be more forthcoming regarding her future plans!

TIME SCALES?

What time scales are we dealing with here, and how long, in the terms of present-day time, would a pole shift take from start to finish? This would depend on (a) the cause, (b) the lead-up and (c) the position into which the planet is moved as a result. It would not, of course, be the first time in the history of man that our planet has turned on its axis and it will not be the last. After all, mankind is a fairly recent phenomenon as far as the history and life-span of the Earth is concerned and, like the dinosaurs, from Danuih's point of view we may well have outworn our welcome.

If this sounds all too much like a prophecy of doom take heart. Pole shifts have been lived through before and, once the dust of disaster settles, as it most certainly will, we could be faced with a new world peopled by a more highly evolved and spiritually mature race of beings. And if Danuih's new field frequency accelerates, as many psychics and metaphysicists suspect, only finer 'fields' (older or more cosmically mature psyches) will be able to pass through it into birth. The 'might is right' syndrome will finally disappear from Danuih's torn and much abused body, the meek will inherit the Earth and the Lion lie with the Lamb; we will have finally reached our Golden Age.

ENDNOTES:

(1) White, J. *Pole Shift*, p. 34.
(2) Edwards, T. *Quantum Domains, Chaos and Fractogenesis*, page 8.
(3) Lewin, Roger. *Complexity; Life on the edge of chaos*, p. 265.
(4) Hope, M. *Atlantis: Myth or Reality*, pp. 14-15.

Chapter 8

PAST POLE SHIFTS

PORTENTS AND THE AWARENESS FACTOR

Over the past few millennia mankind has grown accustomed
to the concept of both a steady state universe and a stable planetary home. Scientists have tended to foster this doctrine to the
extent that any mention of sudden or violent change constitutes
a heresy which is totally out of keeping with established 'facts'.
However, the subtle fluctuations now being observed in the so-
termed 'constants', as outlined in Chapter 6, must surely serve
as portents of much greater changes that are destined to follow in their wake.

Those people who witnessed the build up and latter effects of
former axis tilts must surely have been faced with similar
phenomena to that which our world is being subjected today.
However, orthodox history does not permit the thought of
highly civilized and technologically advanced societies existing in
prehistoric times, in spite of the evidence that has come to light
in recent years. The sad part is that they really did exist, but
movements effected by Danuih, with help from celestial sources,
obliterated them entirely, leaving only a folk memory of both
their greatness and their inevitable surrender to chaos.

But surely, if these people were such great scientists as folk
memory and mysticism would have us believe, they must have
been faced with portents similar to those we are encountering
today. If so, then why did they not make provision accordingly?
The answer is, they did, well, certainly those who were destined
to survive. They vacated their countries of origin and set up
colonies world wide, places they knew would be safe harbours

during the period of devastation that was to follow. Sometimes these moves were subconsciously orchestrated; or perhaps one might suggest that Danuih decided who and what she wished to retain and alerted the relevant 'fields' or psyches accordingly, although I suspect that her outlook is rather more holistic, the finer details coming within the range of frequency acceptancy or nonacceptancy. In other words, she creates the new environment and we can either adjust to it and stay or, assuming our particle cycle to be incomplete, leave our physical bodies behind and be born again elsewhere in the cosmos.

The question is bound to arise as to how this overall concept might work as far as the individual is concerned. I wonder how many of my readers will have experienced an urge to effect a drastic alteration in their lives? Perhaps they have lived in one place for many years and simply feel the need for a change of scenery, or the idea of a home in a foreign country might suddenly seem attractive. Or maybe the decision is made for them, family commitments, illness, disability etc. demanding an uprooting to a new vista. Much the same thing must surely have happened to those people who did manage to escape prior to the disappearance of or dramatic climatic changes in those lands that Danuih and her cosmic family had it in mind to alter.

Professor Charles Hapgood, whose books on the subject include *Maps of the Ancient Sea Kings*, *Earth's Shifting Crust* and *The Path of the Pole*, has tended to favour the idea of slower pole shifts taking place over long periods of time. In *The Path of the Pole* he has dated the coming of the present great ice sheet as between 10,000 and 15,000 years ago, and suggests that there was a time in the Earth's history when both the Arctic and Antarctic were without ice and possibly peopled by civilizations which possessed advanced knowledge of astronomy and cartography, for starters. He refers to the work of B. G. Tilak, an accomplished Vedic scholar, whose book, *The Arctic Home of the Vedas*, has been republished several times since it first appeared in 1903. After examining the Vedic evidence in great detail Tilak arrived at the conclusion that the Vedic peoples were forced to abandon their polar home with the arrival of the Ice Age, the lands they had formerly inhabited having previously enjoyed a mild climate.

Hapgood, however, argues that as there is *at present* no land at the North Pole the Vedas' original home must surely have been around the South Pole, during a time when that area also enjoyed a mild and easily habitable climate, while suggesting that a voyage from Antarctica to India would have posed far less of a problem than crossing the continent of Asia from north to south via the Himalayas. Hapgood cites the ancient maps which show Antarctica minus its ice as proof of his theory, and those interested are recommended to study his works in greater detail. My use of italics above is prompted by the intuitive idea that there was once far more land around what is now the North Pole, much of which went under during an earlier axis tilt; or perhaps the Vedic writings are correct and their original journey was from *what was then the north to south*, the Earth having actually turned upside down! More questions for Danuih. The polar theme has been further developed by Joscelyn Godwin in his scholarly work *Arktos*, in which he covers the catastrophic, uniformitarian and composite theories in great detail.

To return to the question of people being alerted as to the imminence of an impending catastrophy on a world-wide scale, one can only say that those who are destined to vacate their bodies, should such an event occur, will obviously do so, while those who have either elected in pre-life to stay (their field or psyche having made the decision prior to entering the body which has been programmed accordingly) will subconsciously place themselves in safe positions as did the survivors from past cataclysms.

ANCIENT RECORDS - EGYPT/CHINA

So, let us take a trip into the far distant past and see what we can learn concerning former pole shifts. Herodotus tells us that, while relating to him details of the antiquity of their peoples, the priests of Sais '... also said that during this long succession of centuries,* on four separate occasions, the sun moved from his wonted course, twice rising where he now sets, and twice setting where he now rises.'[1]

References to the Sun rising and setting in positions that differ from the present east/west axis are to be found in many archaic writings. In his *History of China*, Martinus Martini, a Jesuit missionary in those parts, wrote of ancient Chinese records that

*36,620 years according to the *Royal Papyrus of Turin*.

mentioned a time when the sky suddenly began to fall northward and the Sun, Moon and planets changed their courses *after the Earth had been shaken.* Other ancient Egyptian sources also bear witness to this, the tomb of Senmouth, architect to Queen Hatshepsut presenting us with a similar enigma. Of the two star maps painted on the ceiling, one places the cardinal points correctly while in the other they are completely reversed, the indication being that the Earth had at some point in the past experienced a tilt, the memory of which was well recorded in pre-dynastic and subsequent Egyptian records. The Harris Papyrus mentions the Earth being overturned during a cosmic cataclysm, while the Hermitage Papyrus of Leningrad and the Ipuwer Papyrus also confirm similar phenomena. The Zodiacal signs in the famous Zodiac of Denderah are arranged in a spiral and the symbols are easily recognizable. The sign of Leo, however, is placed at the vernal equinox (a position at present occupied by Aries) which suggests a closer examination of the dates involved in the precession of equinoxes might prove fruitful for seekers of pole shifts past.

Further correlation of a world-wide catastrophy is to be found in the ancient Egyptian myth of the Goddess Sekhmet the Powerful, the Lion-headed One. The tale goes that Ra, angered when men rebelled against the statutes of cosmic law by misusing certain 'powers', in order to punish them for their misdeeds, withdrew his divine eye from his forehead and smote the Earth with it. This eye is shown in the relevant hieroglyphics as being synonymous with Sekhmet, considered by some authorities to be a leonine version of Hathor. There were, in fact, two eyes of Ra as might be expected. The left, or lunar eye was the 'Eye of Horus'. The eye that Ra hurled at those who transgressed his laws, however, was his right, or solar eye, as symbolized by the Uraeus or Serpent of Wisdom which adorned the insignia of the ancient Egyptian pharaohs and priesthood. It is also the symbol of the cat goddess Bast who, according to Herodotus, was the twin sister of Horus but who in ancient myth was actually the wife of Ra. It would seem that since some interplay between feline and hominid energies has held sway since earlier times, one cannot help wondering if this will also feature in our future. I must remember to ask Danuih about that, plus many other questions to which this chapter has obviously given rise.

SOUTH AMERICA

From the other side of the Atlantic The *Codex Troanus* and the *Codex Cortesianus* outline the Mu-an tragedy quite clearly. The former, which is preserved in the British Museum, is estimated from the form of writing to be around 5,000 years old, similar in age to the latter which is now in the National Museum of Madrid.

THE HOPI LEGEND

The Hopis have a legend of twin gods Poqanghoya and Palongawhoya, guardians of the north and south axes of the Earth respectively, whose task it is to keep the planet rotating properly. They were, however, ordered by Sotuknang, nephew of the Creator, to leave their posts so that the 'second world' could be destroyed because its people had become evil:

> 'Then the world, with no-one to control it, teetered off balance, spun around crazily, then rolled over twice. Mountains plunged into the sea with a great splash, seas and lakes sloshed over the land; and as the world spun through cold and lifeless space it froze into solid ice.'[2]

There is a parallel here with the Egyptian twin Lion gods Shu and Tefnut. The Egyptian Sun-god, Ra, was referred to as 'Ra of the Two Horizons' (horizons is used in this context as a mathematical term denoting a system of dimensions or frame of reference), the Light Horizon and the Life Horizon assumed to represent the material and spiritual realms. Ra of the Life Horizon was symbolized by a flattened circle or solar disk mounted on the hindquarters of two lions seated back to back.

Over the many centuries during which Egypt played a major role in world affairs this symbology received numerous interpretations. In one context, for example, they were viewed as the two primordial forces of life - desire and fear - while to others they were the gods of yesterday (the past) and today (the present or future). Equally, their back to back position could denote the constant battle between chaos and order, while the weight of the Ra disk (reason and self control or, as I would prefer to call it, the reconciling force between these two opposites) holds them in check. In the 'time' context the orb could also be seen as the solar force that holds our planet in its orbital path and thus creates night and day - the time on our clocks. But, and here we come to the crunch line, should one or both of those lions move their position, even slightly, then the orb (Ra) would adjust accordingly, and we would see the Sun *from a different angle* than we do today. The irony of this philosophy, however, lies in the idea that if desire and fear get the better of us, the energies we emit world-wide will cause Shu and Tefnut to rise and dislodge the disk of Ra. In other words, the thoughts and deeds of the peoples of Earth - how we have treated Danuih - is one of the deciding factors as to whether the poles will shift, the axis will tilt and calamity befall us all! A sobering thought for our present age.

NORTHERN EUROPEAN SOURCES

From the *Oera Linda Book* of the ancient Frisians we have the following description of what must surely be a pole shift or tilt of the Earth's axis:

'During the whole summer the sun had hid behind the clouds, as if unwilling to look upon the earth. There was perpetual calm, and the damp mist hung like a wet sail over the houses and the marshes. The air was heavy and oppressive, and in men's hearts was neither joy nor cheerfulness. In the midst of this stillness the earth began to tremble as if she was dying. The mountains opened to vomit forth fire and flames. Some sank into the bosom of the earth and in other places mountains rose out of the plain. Aldland, called by the seafaring people Atland, disappeared, and the wild waves rose so high over hill and dale that everything was buried in the sea. Many people were swallowed up by the earth, and others who had escaped the fire perished in the water.'[3]

Assuming Atland to have occupied the same position indicated by the ancient Frisian records, off the coast of Scandinavia in the area of the North Sea, it would seem logical that their lands were destroyed at the same time that many other land-masses, prominent in prehistoric times, also met their doom. Since recent dredgings in the North Sea have confirmed the fact that large sections of land in that area sank around 5,000 - 6,000 BC, this brings the last pole shift rather near to known history for comfort unless, of course, someone has got their sums wrong.

It is interesting to note that the above account makes no mention of the approach of a celestial body or any such phenomena, which should not, however, be taken as indicative of the absence of such a player in the empyrean drama, since it could possibly have been visible only from the other side of the globe. For me the most interesting statement from this source is that, following the disaster *the climate changed overnight from subtropical to the colder temperatures experienced in present-day Scandinavia*. Rivers altered their courses, whole forests were burned out, and many other countries were submerged. It was almost three years before these disturbances ceased completely, leaving the land with new contours and an entirely different climate. Perhaps the three-year reference is telling us something germane to our own future?

The Norse *Voluspa* offers further confirmation in the following verses:

Verse 3
Until the sons of Bur raised the ground
Created her, Midgarth, the myth
The sun shone on stone battlements from the south,
The ground turned green and verdant with leek.

Verse 4
From the south the sun, the moon's companion,
Touched the edge of the heavens.
The sun did not know his halls.
The moon did not know her might.
The stars did not know their places.[4]

Here we have a clear allusion to the Sun rising in the south, and to the subsequent displacement of both Sun and Moon, while the question of the Moon being unaware of her might suggests that this body exerted some powerful influence on the events taking place that was totally out of character with its previous role in relation to the celestial balance. The reference to the Sun not knowing his halls and the stars being unaware of their places obviously alludes to their change in position *as seen from the Earth.* It would appear that, not only did the position of the poles change, but the Earth either turned upside down or rolled over, eventually settling into its present position!

GREECE

The ancient Greek sages believed that the Earth underwent periodic reversals of rotation, an uninclined ecliptic being the correct 'way up' for Danuih, and therefore associated with her Golden Age. In Plato's dialogue *The Statesman*, for example, there is mention of the Sun and the planets setting where they now rise and rising where they once set; followed by the explanation that all such tales originated from descriptions of the same cosmic event. Godwin quotes:

'... A shudder passed through the world at the reversing of its rotation, checked as it was between the old control and the new impulse which had turned end into beginning for it and beginning into end.'[5]

Godwin suggests that the Greeks probably culled such ideas from scientifically more advanced cultures such as those of Chaldea and Egypt who (I would suggest), in turn, inherited them from Atlantean settlers.

BRITAIN

It was not until the science of astronomy blossomed in the seventeenth century that certain scholars started to effect a relationship between a Golden Age and polar inclination. John Milton, writing in *Paradise Lost* (completed 1665) mentioned how God actually employed a pole shift to bring the Edenic state to an end:

'Some say he bid his angels turne askance
The Poles of Earth twice ten degrees and more

From the Sun's Axle; they with labour push'd
Oblique the Centric Globe

... to bring in change
Of Seasons to each Clime: else had the Spring
Perpetual smil'd on Earth with vernant Flours,
Equal in Days and Nights, except for those
Beyond the Polar Circles ...' [6]

Godwin also mentions two English divines who, later in that century, also concluded that God effected a pole shift in order to change the status of mankind and all living creatures. Thomas Burnet's (1635-1715) *Sacred Theory of the Earth* (1681), and William Whitson's (1667-1752) *New Theory of the Earth* both explore, among other things, the pole shift theory in relation to the restoration of polar equilibrium (inclination) eventually resulting in the return of a Golden Age, the last pole shift having catapulted the Earth and all thereon into a period of suffering and chaos (the wages of sin in their eyes, no doubt!).

However, I could not hope to do justice to the fruits of Godwin's erudition, and those requiring more details are recommended to read *Arktos* for themselves.

THE ICE AGE THEORY

In considering the causes of both changes of climate and the movements of peoples in prehistoric times one must, of course, take into account the question of Ice Ages and their relevance to our text. In 1836, Swiss naturalist Louis Agassiz persuaded Professor Jean Charpentier to accompany him to an Alpine glacier to demonstrate to him the fallacy of the new idea that Europe was once covered entirely by ice. Upon arrival at the edge of the glacier, Agassiz, the sceptic, was himself converted and later became the chief apostle of the new theory. Basing his conclusions on observations also made in other parts of the world and, after demonstrations to the leading authorities of the day which ultimately won their support, he published his theory in a work entitled *Etudes sur les glaciers* (1840).It contained the following statement on p.314:

'The surface of Europe previously adorned with tropical vegetation and populated by herds of huge elephants, enormous hippopotami, and gigantic carnivora, was suddenly buried under a vast mantle of ice, covering planes, lakes, seas, and plateaux. Upon the life and movement of a vigorous creation fell the silence of death. Springs vanished, rivers ceased flowing, the rays of the sun, rising upon this frozen shore (if indeed they reached it), encountered only the breath of winter from the north and the thunder of crevasses as they opened up across the surfaces of this icy sea.' [7]

Both the commencement and ending of the Ice Age were therefore viewed by Agassiz as catastrophic events, the suddenness of the ice invasion being evident in the mammoths of Siberia, who were caught so rapidly in the sudden deep freeze as to preserve them and their meal of fresh buttercup-laden grass for posterity. In commenting on the mammoth phenomenon in Siberia former rocket scientist Dr. Otto Muck suggests:

'To find trees like these that supplied food for mammoths in the Ice Age one would have to go further south, to the region of Lake Baikal, to travel the same distance as the North Pole possibly shifted in the Atlantic catastrophe. The primeval forest receded southward as the North Pole shifted North.' [8]

Agassiz' Tertiary estimate for the Ice Age was later corrected by the British geologist Sir Charles Lyell (1797-1875) who placed it in the Pleistocene or Quarternary Period, which is characterized by the alternate appearance and recession of northern glaciation and the appearance of the progenitors of man.

In more recent times, however, researchers have offered more precise dates; Muck, for example, who submitted the following table:

Period	Sub-period	Beginning about	Type of climate
Quarternary	Würm glacial	20,000 BC	typically glacial
	Epiglacial	10,000 BC	sub-boreal (raw, cold)
Quinternary	Post-glacial	5,000 BC	optimum climate
	Present	2,000 BC	decreasing warmth

Source: Otto Muck, *The Secret of Atlantis*, Fred Bradley (trs), London. William Collins Sons & Co. 1978, p.67.

Mammoths, we are told, lived in the Quarternary Age and became extinct in the Quinternary Age, having clearly been destroyed in some sudden, major catastrophe.

That there was an Ice Age is clearly stated by the geological evidence. But what if the whole planet had been in a slightly different position in relation to the Sun, so that some areas that had formerly been warm were overtaken by ice, and others exposed to a warmer temperature? This would also accord with the pole theory proffered by Hapgood.

Robert Scrutton draws our attention to Richard Mooney's comment regarding the last Ice Age, the Würm. At its maximum extent the ice field covered the British Isles as far south as the Thames Valley, North America as far south as the Mississippi Delta, and parts of Scandinavia, France, Germany and Russia. However, it appears to have missed Jutland (Denmark) and spread no further west than Mecklenburg in East Germany while a large part of Siberia escaped. This raises the questions why there is no evidence of a similar spread of ice at the South Pole and why are the kind of geological conditions normally associated with glaciations absent in the present Arctic regions?[9] The movements of ice-sheets usually cause striations (scratches) on rock surfaces. In the Highlands of Scotland, where the evidence of glaciation is most noticeable, there are striations on the north-facing slopes, while on the south-facing slopes there are none. It would be logical to assume that the ice moving down from the north, having ascended the hill slopes on one side, would have made an even deeper impression on the other.

Mooney, in fact, suggests that there never was a world-wide Ice Age as such; what happened was that the polar regions simply shifted, bringing glaciation to lands that were once temperate and thus exposing formerly colder regions to a milder climate. I have to say I agree with him.

MU AND ATLANTIS

Sizeable shifts in the Earth's crust due, no doubt, to axis tilts, have been well documented and discussed. For example, the British scientist Blandford was of the opinion that both physical geography and palaeontology unanimously confirmed the existence of Mu (also named Lemuria by another British scientist, P. Sclater, who saw this continent as the cradle of humankind and called it after the Lemurs) from the beginning of the so-called Permian epoch until the end of the Miocene Period. Other scientists, however, have dated the Mu-an catastrophy near 15,000 B.C. which coincides with Hapgood's assessment of the beginning of a sizeable shift in the Earth's crust. For those subscribing to the Atlantis theory, this would have given the Atlantean people some 6,000 to 7,000 years in which to build up their civilization to the status it is believed to have achieved prior to its own disappearance during the last pole shift.[10]

Theories as to the final sinking of Atlantis, which are too numerous to recount here, are well covered in my two books on the subject: *Atlantis: Myth or Reality* and *Practical Atlantean Magic*. In the former I was commissioned to pursue a strictly empirical and highly researched approach while the latter allowed me to meander into metaphysical and mythological considerations. The Bibliographies supplied in both works provide a comprehensive list of reading matter on the subject.

POSSIBLE CAUSES

White's list of possible reasons is given in the previous chapter and, as he points out, any of several phenomena could cause a planet to flip over or change its angle of axis. It could, for example, be struck by an extra-terrestrial body such as an asteroid, comet or planetesimal, as suggested by Otto Muck in *The Secret of Atlantis*.

Equally plausible is Professor Hans Hoerbiger's lunar theory, in which he suggested that, prior to acquiring its present satellite, our planet had a small tertiary moon which was eventually drawn into the Earth's orbit, the resulting catastrophy being responsible for the sinking of the aforementioned vast landmass of Mu (Lemuria) in the Pacific ocean. Mu is believed to have occupied a large area between South America and Asia which originally encompassed Hawaii to the north, Easter Island to the south east and Tonga to the west. Its remnants are still to be found in the numerous groups of islands which bespatter that area of the Pacific. [11] According to Hoerbiger, it was the acquisition of our present Moon which precipitated the axis tilt that sent Atlantis to the bottom of the ocean.

Colonel A. Braghine, writing in *The Shadow of Atlantis*, stated that the ancient Greeks were well acquainted with Hoerbiger's theory regarding a Preselenite Age, as well as being fully cognizant of the natural cycle of pole shifts that forms part of the normal growth and development of our planet. Hoerbiger's theories were also well supported by H. S. Bellamy and, in more recent times, the French scholar Professor Denis Saurat.

Having established from past sources that Danuih's proposed pole shift is logically feasible since it represents no more than a natural cyclic phenomenon, I think the time has come to hand over to her for her comments on this and other issues of interest and importance to all of us who reside on and about her surface.

ENDNOTES:

(1) Schwaller de Lubicz, R.A. *Sacred Science*, p.87.
(2) Goodman, J. *The Earthquake Generation*, pp. 160-161.
(3) Scrutton, R. *The Other Atlantis*, p.48.
(4) Muck, O. *The Secret of Atlantis*, p.176.
(5) Godwin, J. *Arktos*, pp. 182-184.
(6) *Ibid*, Muck, p. 176.
(7) Velikovsky, I. *Earth In Upheaval*, p.34.
(8) *Ibid*, Muck, page 220.
(9) *Ibid*, Scrutton, p.50.
(10) Hope, M. *Atlantis: Myth or Reality?*, p.116.
(11) Hope, M. *Practical Atlantean Magic*, p.16.

Chapter 9

DANUIH'S VERSION

POLE SHIFTS PAST AND PRESENT

M: Well, Danuih, I think the time has come for us to resume our dialogue, the last chapter having certainly raised some interesting queries. So, shall we start with those first?

D: Why not?

M: Were the Egyptian priests correct in the information they gave to Herodotus regarding the number of times you have shifted your poles in the past?

D: From the human angle, yes, but overall, no. Prior to the advent of the human race I shifted my position several times but as this epoch is irrelevant to your inquiry (humankind only seems to concern itself with the effects of pole shifts on its own species), let us give the Egyptian priests some credit for the accuracy of their statement.

M: Regarding past pole shifts; have these always been of the same magnitude?

D: Good gracious no. Some have been minimal while others have involved a complete reversal.

M: My scientist friends seem to think you have something like 90 or even 180 degrees in mind for your next axis tilt. Is this correct?

D: The extent to which I shift is not entirely dependent on me. Other factors need to be taken into consideration as the severity (or otherwise) of my quantum leap will affect the rest of the solar system as well as my mother. In other words, it will result from a joint effort that will effect changes for all parties concerned.

M: But surely you must have some idea as to your future?

D: You credit me with being a Time Lord, an exalted position from which I am at present far removed. As any genuine human psychic could verify when endeavouring to view the future, the finer details, and time, are extremely difficult to pinpoint. Only when these have been agreed at loftier levels (you have a saying 'as above, so below') are the seers able to deliver their messages with any degree of accuracy. To ascertain how decisions will be made within faster frequencies one needs to have access to the point at which all time merges - the realm of the Time Lords. However, to give you a clue, my body will ultimately end up in the position it occupied during your so-termed 'Golden Age'.

M: Thank you for the tip. I have visions of Atlantis at the height of its glory, long before the chaos set in!

D: Perhaps, but, remember, experience is never repeated *exactly*. The subject of psychic probing begs me to comment on the attitude many so-termed 'believers' among humankind adopt towards any spirit (field) that happens to be non-local, or what you term out of 'incarnation'. The assumption that a young soul or limited field suddenly acquires all knowledge upon parting with its body seems totally illogical to me. And yet many people will take as gospel any information purporting to come from sources external to those computable by their five senses. Time Lords have, on occasions, condescended to dwell among humankind and suffer accordingly but, needless to say, they are seldom recognized at the time, humankind generally preferring to follow either someone who puts on a display that would do credit to a media magician, or any teacher likely to flatter their personal egos. Sister, why don't you

produce that appropriate quote which I am accessing in
your databanks ...?

M: I think I know the one you mean. It concerns the Gnostic
classification of the Hyle, Psyche and Pneuma. I quote from
the Victorian scholar, G. R. S. Mead:

> '(a) ... the lowest, or *hylics*, were those who were so en-
> tirely dead to spiritual things that they were as the *hyle*
> or unperceptive matter of the world; (b) the intermedi-
> ate class were called *psychics*, for though believers in
> things spiritual, they were believers simply, and required
> miracles and signs to strengthen their faith; (c) whereas
> the *pneumatics* or spiritual, the highest class, were those
> capable of knowledge of spiritual matters, those who
> could receive the Gnosis.'

Mead continues:

> 'It is somewhat the custom in our days in extreme cir-
> cles to claim that all men are "equal". The modern
> theologian wisely qualifies the claim by the adverb "mor-
> ally". Thus stated the idea is by no means a peculiarly
> Christian view - for the doctrine is common to all great
> religions, seeing that it simply asserts the great principle
> of justice as one of the manifestations of the Deity. The
> Gnostic view, however, is far clearer and more in accord
> with the facts of evolution; it admits the "morally equal",
> but it further asserts difference of degree, not only in
> body and soul, but also in spirit, in order to make the
> morality proportional and so carry out the inner mean-
> ing of the parable of the talents.' [1]

M: I assumed you wanted the whole piece?

D: You assumed correctly. Can you not see how Mead's summary accords with the field theory?

M: Yes, indeed. But then I've never been one to believe in
equality, as you well know. To me the world-scenario should
be more in keeping with the principle of harmony than that

of unison. Surely many *different* notes making up the symphony of life is infinitely preferable to a mass group of clones?

ON RELIGION

D: Quite so. However, while we are on this subject, I suppose I had better tie in the ends regarding religion, as you seem to have committed me for this one in earlier chapters.

M: Yes, please.

D: I am asked whether I believe in, or accept as valid, any of the great religions currently favoured by humankind. The question amuses me inasmuch as that I am not a hominid and as such do not require a spiritual strap upon which to hang. Nor am I afflicted by the great sense of fear and insecurity that pervades the majority of the human race. Their religions I liken to chess pieces in the hominid ego game, since most of them encourage humankind to view itself as greater, more evolved, and more powerful than any of the other species to which I give succour. Those faiths which aim to separate humankind from the implicate whole, of which it constitutes only one minute fraction, are abhorrent to me since they neither acknowledge my existence as an entity in my own right, nor accept the consciousness, and therefore comparative suffering, of those other species that exist on and around my surface. The tragedy lies in the fact that those who, in following such beliefs are guilty of inflicting pain on what you term 'lesser' creatures, will have to pay for their misdeed if not in my aura then on some other chaotic planet somewhere else in the universe.

M: Do you share the view espoused by some hominids that the great religious teachers themselves were 'on the right track' but that, following their deaths, their teachings were conveniently rehashed for political or other devious reasons?

D: I cannot agree that all those responsible for founding the major religions were guilt-free since some of them were decidedly on ego trips. However, as I have no wish that you should incur the wrath of their followers I shall refrain from giving any names. There were, however, genuine seekers among them who did their sincere best to bring enlightenment, and I'll leave the readers to work that one out for themselves.

M: Have any of the great teachers been Time Lords incarnate?

D: To my knowledge, and I accept that this is limited, Time Lords only incarnate at certain times for specific reasons which are not necessarily anything to do with religion or mystical teachings. What they are involved with, however, are inter-cosmic events which influence not only my orb and those dwelling thereon and therein but also other celestial bodies. What people must understand is that when any particle, be it as minute as a quark or as large as Jupiter, effects a quantum leap, this sends out ripples of energy in much the same way as if you drop a stone into a pond. Therefore, many, many fields, be they accompanying particles (with bodies) or simply waves in non-locality, are affected by it. When an event of this kind is due to take place you may be sure that both the Time Lords and their progeny are around somewhere. The last time a Time Lord took a body on my surface was in a civilization you know as Atlantis, which disappeared during my last major quantum leap.

ON GOD

M: The existence of a single, supreme deity seems to be the most popularly espoused belief in most religious circles today. Any comments?

D: All 'fields' (and that goes for hominids and planetary bodies) are gods in the making and, since the function of a deity, even an infant one, is creativity, the developing field and its accompanying particle (body) starts 'having a go' at this from an early spiritual age. Perspective among humankind being limited due to a lack of genuine cosmic guidance, however, most of their creations are simply mirror images of aspects of themselves. What happens is this: as you have previously explained, those people who encounter an energy field, which their right brain acknowledges but for which their left brain has no terms of reference, automatically clothe it in an image of the familiar which will be based on their religious, philosophic or humanistic programming. For example, an ancient patriachal tribe espousing the concept of a single supreme deity would naturally tend to visualize it as a male of similar appearance to their own leaders or patriarchs. Sadly, images of this kind persisted down the centuries, having become stuck in the recorded groove of those later followers who are unable to rationalize the iconographical effect of the conditions prevailing at the time of that religion's inception.

The acceleration in the energies on and around my body is producing some strange effects on humankind. Those fields (souls) too immature to handle these frequency increases are turning to violence as the only outlet via which to express them. In others, the escalation in consciousness is over-emphasizing the creative mode, resulting in the conjuration of a series of religious gurus, space contacts, galactic 'councils' and a host of other, aforementioned extra-terrestrial images which constitute nothing more than humankind's youthful attempts to create replicas of its own species elsewhere in the cosmos. The surfeit of channellers supposedly bringing through Jesuses, Michaels, Masters various, etc. and other characters from the scriptures of your major religions has added to the confusion, much of the information offered being contradictory! But then people cannot say they were not warned; even those very scriptures to which many adhere tell of false prophets. The sad fact is that only parts of the original teachings were correct, and much of that has been jettisoned over the ages in favour of more politically or sociologically accepted tenets.

As to my own concept of what you call God, of course it cannot be a single divinity since it has to be made up of an infinite number of cells each with its own distinct flavour and understanding. Unlike many humans I have no delusions regarding a 'hot-line' to such a divinity, but those older and wiser than I hint that it has something to do with Time and therefore the Time Lords, or 'Old Ones' as you prefer to call them, sister, which I will come to know and experience for myself in the fullness of my evolutionary cycle. Someone recently asked me if I had ever made a ghostly appearance in humanoid form to give guidance and light and if not, why not? I replied that I had, on several occasions, but since (in recent years, anyway) replicas of my visitations reached no further than alcoves in Catholic churches I gave up. After all, I don't look like that anyway and, were I to appear to someone as a spheroid of light, I would probably be accused of being a UFO!

Another 'New Age' phenomenon which is incompatible with my own understanding is the 'sweetness and light' idea that there is no such thing as chaos (referred to as 'evil' by humankind since that is how it tends to manifest via the hominid condition). The order/chaos sequence is and always will be with us all; our development as individual fields being dependent upon the way we deal with the precarious balance between the excesses of chaos and the restrictions of order. Much as groups of New Age and religiously orientated goody-goodies (have I got that one right, sister, or am I selecting the wrong term from your databanks?), intent upon bringing light to the world and halting my quantum leap, pray hard to their deity to retain the present *status quo*, the natural alternation between order and chaos will inevitably take place. After all, the very deity that they pray to is believed to have made the rules in the first place, so why should It break them to suit their whims?

M: You have reminded me of the words of Vera Stanley Alder, a mage of this century, who commented, 'God does not reverse his Law of Gravity to prevent one person from committing suicide by jumping from a high place' (my recollection of the wording may be incorrect as this is not a direct quote), the inference being, what would happen to all those the right way up if He did!

D: An excellent example. One wonders why people cannot see this.

ATLANTIS

M: You mentioned Atlantis earlier, and how a Time Lord once incarnated there. If Atlantis was favoured by such a powerful visitation, why did it have to go?

D: Atlantis was ahead of its time, its technological achievements alone being as yet unsurpassed. Unfortunately, once it opened its portals to the rest of the world, such powers fell into the hands of those insufficiently wise (unevolved) to handle them; so, in a way, the resultant admixture of original Atlanteans and incoming barbarians effected its own destruction via the process of accelerated entropy associated by your scientists with the Second Law of Thermodynamics. As to the appearance there of a Time Lord, I am told that Time Lords always take on bodies to aid quantum leaps in particular species; in other words, they introduce the relative gene into the DNA of a particular race which is then distributed globally. This fact, which was known to the priesthoods of several ancient civilizations as well as the elders of certain tribes which can be dated back to antiquity, gave rise to the myth of the 'divine ancestor'.

M: Is that what is happening in the world today and will we all be witnessing the advent of another Time Lord?

D: The answer to the first part of your question is, not really. Today your problem is worldwide; in Atlantean times it was contained and therefore easy to eliminate without causing a global conflagration. Besides, the virus which pervades my body has now spread and the time has come to effect a good clean-out. There will be no physical visitation from a Time Lord, of that I have been assured, although what will happen is that such a Being will supervise the takeover of my guidance and assist with the final elimination of the virus. As I have previously explained, the Egyptians were correct in their surmise that all fields are in turn guided by other fields or energies and, therefore, a new influence will overshadow me once my position has been adjusted.

THE VIRUS

M: Could you tell us more about this virus? The Crystal People told me about it some time ago and I have often been asked to elucidate.

D: Naughty, naughty! You know more about the virus than I do but I can understand your reluctance to be forthcoming. After all, as I have already mentioned, humankind tends to pay far more attention to the words of extra-terrestrials, the spirits of those who have achieved renown in your past, or even the ghost of late departed Auntie Flo, than anyone at present in particle form or, to use your own term, incarnate. So, for the benefit of your readers, I will tell you that such agents of chaos which are constantly passing through space and time represent problems or difficulties that have to be overcome before the next stage in spiritual development (which I prefer to view as an acceleration in frequency) can be attained. Look at it this way: when anyone has a virus they naturally feel very ill. Not only are they consciously aware of their discomfort, but all the other life forms to which they are host also suffer with them. Translate this into terms of a planet and its inhabitants and you have your answer.

M: It does seem to me that, when it comes to the question of the virus affecting people, some have suffered more than others.

D: Not really, although both sexes have been differently affected. Besides, it should also be borne in mind that each and every person has his or her own development to consider (you say 'karma') and all are in different stages of spiritual growth. No officiating deity forced anyone to be born into such conditions; those of humankind who are still bound by the hominid group soul (have not as yet individuated) were drawn into them because like attracts like, while the remainder have elected to undergo the experiences offered in order to learn to cope with the subtle balance between chaos and order. The real sufferers in this nightmarish drama have been those helpless creatures upon which humankind has practised such terrible cruelties - creatures which have more of a right to live out their lives on and around my surface, according to the nature of their species, than humankind. But then I blame your religions for much of this, which remark might give you some idea as to the answer to the question you raised earlier.

CONCERNING GENDER

M: Since you have raised the subject of gender could you tell us why hominids on your surface suffer from this gender problem or 'battle of the sexes' as it is called?

D: The virus has exerted a profound effect on both males and females, one manifestation of its malignance being the hostility and lack of understanding between members of the sexes which it has tended to exaggerate. In a highly evolved society such differences would not exist since, in the hominid species, the mental and physical gap between male and female naturally decreases with evolution. The genetic make-up of the male tends to over-emphasize aggression, especially in uninformed fields (younger souls to you) while the effect on the female has been predominantly hormonal. An accentuated libido is, I regret to say, a sign of spiritual youth!

The erroneous myth of the superiority of either sex needs to be expunged. Your scientists have recently stated that female brains compensate for their smaller size by working faster than those of men, while men's brains deteriorate three times faster than those of women. However, the usage made of the brain is far more important than its physical size and, believe it or not, the size of the head and therefore the brain is no indication of intelligence in humankind or any other species in the universe. So much for the spate of large-headed aliens of superior intelligence that seem to appear with regularity to UFO contactees. All highly questionable by my standards, but then I *am* actually aware of what comes and goes from my orbit and whence some of it originates.

EGYPT AND SIRIUS

M: Did any of the ancient civilizations that came after Atlantis possess real knowledge of the cosmos and how it functions?

D: Those places colonized by the Atlanteans carried a vestige of the old truths for many years, although ultimately these were abandoned in favour of more materially satisfying precepts. The ancient Egyptians retained a knowledge of my ancestors for many years, and built their edifices in alignment with the time-star Sirius, while also showing how the energies were transferred via the Orion complex to my family here in this solar system. The more enlightened among them were also aware of the life-force in all things, plus the fact that more highly evolved energy fields were not confined to either any particular cosmic species, or to the image and likeness of any one manifestation of life on or around my surface. They went way off beam with mummification, however, the materialistic aspect having taken too firm a hold of them over the centuries.

TIME

M: You mention time travellers entering and departing via Sirius: one immediately conjures up a picture of some fictional character from the world of entertainment, seated comfortably in his or her appropriate contraption with coordinates set for the next dimension. Now you and I both know this is not the case, but a comment would, I am sure, be appreciated.

D: Just as your X-rays pass through your body unfelt and un-seen by the naked eye so also do subtle fields move undetected (except by even subtler fields) from universe to universe. Humankind should really make an effort to stop visualizing everything in its own image and likeness. A field in non-locality is, as has already been explained, form-less unless encapsulated in a time warp (see Chapter 1). Regarding the Time Lords to which I am inclined to refer, these are simply very subtle, powerful fields of energy of such fine frequencies that they can pass instantaneously from universe to universe at will. In fact, there is no time involved at all in their transition; they simply 'exist' in all time simultaneously and are thus aware of all that takes place therein. There are, however, many fields of consciousness that have not yet achieved the status of Time Lord but who are conversant with time as a source of energy and how to negotiate and utilize it. It is such beings as these who use the entrances and exits, provided by stars such as Sirius, to negotiate those universes that function within the scope of their own wave-bands.

M: As you well know, I have written a book in which I proposed that Time was an energy in itself and as such constituted the fifth or unifying force along with those already established by science (weak and strong nuclear forces, electromagnetism and gravity). Can you shed any light on this? Am I, in fact, 'up the proverbial creek'?

D: I shall refrain from expressing annoyance with you at this question and you know well the reason why. Of course Time is an energy. Without Time there would be no universe and no you and I. But surely you are not alone in this idea. For the benefit of the reader why not give the names of others who have arrived at the same conclusion?

M: Well, J. W. Dunne was one and, more recently, the Russian astronomer Pulkovo Koryzer (born 1908), who put forward a theory (since the last war) which he entitled *Causal Mechanics*, the main theme of which is that the flow of time is the main energy source of the stars. Unfortunately for Koryzer, Stalin took a dim view of his ideas and he met his end in one of the tyrant's famous 'purges'. Astronomer Patrick Moore commented on Koryzer's work in his book, *The Armchair Astronomer*, but dismissed the Time idea - it was probably too far removed from the rigid orthodox approach for which Moore is so well known.

D: Would it be any comfort for you to know that said Russian has now been born into another body and, come maturity, is hell-bent upon proving the theory once and for all (not that it will need much proving in the years to come).

M: I am absolutely delighted. I suppose you would not happen to know into which country he has come?

D: Your own, actually, and it is a 'she' and not a 'he'!

LOVELOCK'S HYPOTHESIS

M: Professor Sir James Lovelock has surely brought your plight to public notice with his *Gaia Hypothesis*. How do you feel about that?

D: Lovelock certainly tumbled to what I am up to, in keeping with several others who have recently written books indicating that I am 'sick' as they term it. He fails to credit me with intelligence, however, which does not concern me in the least since I fully intend to do my own thing anyway. Besides, he will find out sooner or later. At least I owe him a great deal for exposing my predicament to a species totally insensitive to my existence, let alone my pain.

HEALTH

M: Since your original mission as a planet was to promote healing and music, or balance and harmony as you prefer, does the excess of illness among all creatures on your surface not bother you?

D: Naturally. But what can a doctor do about it when he or she is also ill? I have to say, however, that humankind brings on a lot of its illness itself without any help from the virus. A typical example of this is in the food eaten which in most cases is totally inappropriate to the design of the hominid body. If people observed this fact they would live much longer and be much healthier. There is a saying among humans 'you are what you eat' which could not be truer. Those who stuff themselves with rubbish are likely to attract rubbish; but perhaps we have a 'chicken and egg' situation here since like inevitably attracts like. It should also be borne in mind that there are diseases arising not only from an excess of chaos *but also from an excess of order*, if you would care to work that one out, while another factor contributory to ill health is humankind's lack of regard for the minute species that live on or in their bodies. Someone recently accused me of failing to take into consideration the suffering I could cause if I shift my poles; my reply was 'Do you consult all the life-forms that live on your body prior to effecting a decision in your life?'

Excesses of any kind are guaranteed to cause ill health. Were humans able to control themselves sufficiently to live within the limitations imposed by that aggregate of particles they call their body, in other words live in balance, they would enjoy much better health all round, virus or no virus. In fact, by denying the need for moderation in all things they are actually leaving themselves wide open to the worst possible viral effects, some of which are already out of all proportion, at which point I will cease at the boundary of that delicate line defined by 'political correctness'.

THE SHADOW

M: Danuih, I wrote about your Shadow in an earlier chapter. Any comments?

D: I am sometimes extremely angry and this precipitates my punitive, destructive side. Your mythologists write of 'the wrath of the gods' being responsible for past pole shifts or axis tilts. I have to confess to feeling such wrath, but I am not a god. My elemental family and I do, however, have strength superior to anything humankind can come up with which we shall not hesitate to use to our advantage in the future. However, I am obliged to wait for the green light; but let me put it this way, the amber is showing right now!

THE ARCHETYPAL WORLDS

M: Former references to archetypes and the archetypal worlds surely call for your comments. Such figures as the archetypal mother, father, healer, warrior, etc. are obvious, but it has been requested of me that I ask you to elucidate on the sacrificial saviour; surely this archetype will not form part of your brave new world?

D: One should not confuse obvious personality disorders with genuine self-sacrifice. But, people will ask, how can one effect a distinction? A little hominid psychology, based on persistent observation, will help here. Archetypal saviours/ sufferers are often self-mutilants, or they invite mutilation by others in order to act out a role such as that of the sacrificial victim. Sorry, sister, but to explain this in detail would require more knowledge than you possess. Could you help me by recommending the correct reading matter for those interested?

M: Certainly. What about *Diagnostic and Statistical Manual of Mental Disorders* (Third Edition - Revised), published by The American Psychiatric Association, Washington, D. C. This gives a comprehensive analysis of all personality disorders. I expect there is also a British equivalent but I just happen to have a copy of the above, a present from a dear friend across the 'pond'. I would reproduce parts of it here but the language is somewhat too technical for people outside the disciplines of psychology or psychiatry. Besides, it does go on a bit!

D: Personality disorders often abound in religious circles where they are sometimes viewed as evidence of sanctity. In centuries past they were often accepted as manifestations of the divine, as was epilepsy, so it is little wonder that the mutilated shaman or sacrificed saviour figure attracted large followings. In today's world, however, such manifestations would be more likely to attract the men in white coats than an adoring following although, however, the general reactions of humankind, and their following instinct in particular, never cease to amaze me!

ASTROLOGY

M: Danuih, can you comment on the study and application of astrology?

D: No problem. You have the attributes (and shadows!) of my family fairly neatly tied up although you are actually two planets short, there being no need for the double allocations to Mercury and Venus. But since that enigma will eventually be resolved by your astronomers I am happy to leave it in their capable hands.

   More attention should, however, be paid to the influence exerted by what you term 'fixed stars', on both the planets themselves and life on my body generally; and I wonder how many people have tumbled to the fact that I, and not my satellite, am what would be termed the 'ruler' of that area of the heavens designated by your astrologers as the zodiacal sign of Cancer? You should really dispense with the term 'ruler', the inferred relationship being more of an affinity or shared influence. Neither is my mother the 'ruler° of Leo. Then who is, you may ask? Wait and see what the future unfolds and then you will know, although some have already put two and two together and arrived at the correct answer.

M: As an astrologer I find this all very interesting. I suppose it is logical to assume that you, as a water planet, should be associated with Cancer, but then astrologers seldom take you into consideration when designating planetary/zodiacal partnerships.

D: That is true. But now I am going to suggest that we stop at this point; firstly, because you are tiring, which begins to make communication a little difficult and, secondly, because I think we have covered sufficient subject matter for you to analyse in the ensuing days.

ENDNOTES:

(1) Mead, G.R.S. *Fragments of a Faith Forgotten*, pp.139-140.

Chapter 10

FURTHER ANALYSIS AND CORRELATION

The wide range of subject matter covered in the last chapter has left me once again with the onerous task of commentary and substantiation if, indeed, the latter is possible as far as some of the information is concerned. However, we will do what we can with what we have. Regarding the pole shift, my mind is still loaded with unanswered questions: the survival factor, for example. What percentage of the world's population would be left after Danuih has effected her quantum leap; how long will things take to settle down again into the new climate, etc.; will we move nearer to or further from the Sun; will there be more or less days in a year or a similar adjustment in hours in the day; how does the Greenhouse Effect fit in with all this? Questions, questions. And what about the myriad prophecies that are coming through thick and fast - do they all constitute a part of the 'end of millennium hysteria'?

THE SUBTLE EFFECTS OF MAGNETIC AND OTHER PHYSICAL CHANGES

What we can gather from Danuih's answers is that subtle changes taking place in the Earth's magnetic field are responsible for the escalating breakdown in law and order, while also effecting a sorting of the 'wheat from the chaff' in society worldwide. Danuih's comments concerning these observable effects could be aligned with aforementioned fluctuations in the Earth's electromagnetic and gravitational fields which would in turn actuate electrical neuronal responses in the brain, the resulting cerebral repercussions accounting for the exaggerated behavioural patterns that are adding daily to the crime rate.

It seems pretty clear that the massive doses of radiation that will result from interactions between changing electrical/magnetic/gravitational fields will cause genetic mutations in all surviving life-forms so, as Danuih has suggested, survival will very much depend on the individual's ability to adjust to the incoming energies.

DANUIH'S OWN BELIEFS AND CONDEMNATIONS

Danuih talks a lot about the Time Lords which leads me to the conclusion that they represent to her what God represents to many people here on her surface. In that respect, and as a pananimist, I have to admit to being on her side of the fence.

What I do find rather scary is her denouncement of the flood of channelled and similar forecasts which are pervading the metaphysical scene at present. Having examined some of these in detail one wonders how rational people could be taken in by such tin-pot gurus, be they incarnate or discarnate. After the Koresh episode, however, one cannot fail to see her viewpoint: humankind is totally irrational at times, in spite of its myth of superiority! Another aspect of this that springs to mind is that of the unscrupulous racketeers who, posing as prophets or gurus, cash in on frightened people who, believing that the end is nigh, hastily and foolishly dispose of their worldly possessions into eager, waiting hands.

THE SONS OF GOD AND DAUGHTERS OF MEN?

I was particularly intrigued by the piece about alterations in DNA being effected by a visit from a Time Lord. I suppose what happens is that such a personage passes on this gene to the children he or she produces by cohabiting with those around him/her, be they wives or otherwise. Oh dear, I think we are coming back full circle to the 'sons of god and daughters of men' bit from the Bible, and other 'divine ancestor' myths! No smoke without fire, as they say. In my efforts to logicize this one I can conceive of the implanted genes being passed around the globe over thousands of years, until they have reached the number of people destined to come through the next evolutionary quantum leap in one piece: the wheat as against the chaff? I have always been aware of the existence of the Sirius gene; now I know how it came here and who brought it. Also, how to recognize those who carry it. From what has been said I gather this will be the last phase in the evolution of humankind on Danuih's body, after which she will again shift her poles to a position that will no longer allow her to support the hominid species.

DANUIH'S EVENTUAL DEMISE

Interestingly enough Lovelock has something to say about this, although he tends to agree with Danuih that the end of the world as such is a long, long way away. Scientists have been toying with possible apocalyptic scenarios for many years; here are a few of them: Richard Wade-Martins of Cambridge University, runner-up in the Telegraph Young Science Writer Awards, 1993 (I quote with permission from their Science Column), tells us:

> 'If the Earth were to hit an object measuring 440 km across travelling at 38,000 mph (the approach velocity of present asteroids), the impact would generate enough energy to vaporise all the oceans. The Earth would be enveloped by a cloud of steam at 1,200 degrees C which would take 3,000 years to cool down, by which time all life on Earth would have been annihilated.
>
> 'Another scenario for the end of life on Earth was recently suggested by two American Earth scientists at Pennsylvania State University, Ken Calderia and James Kasting. They were building on previous work involving the British scientist, James Lovelock, proposer of the Gaia hypothesis.
>
> 'In 1982 Lovelock co-wrote a paper in *Nature* predicting that life on Earth would come to an end in around 100 million years' time, which geologically is a mere shake of a lamb's tail. Life on Earth arose about 3,500 million years ago and, if Lovelock were right, we would have only three per cent of life's allotted time left to run. What could be the cause of this end?

'As the Sun grows older, it will grow hotter and brighter, which in turn will warm up our own planet. As our planet gets hotter, there will be an increase in the chemical weathering of silicate rocks on the Earth's surface. This weathering reaction absorbs carbon dioxide, and so, in a warming climate, the level of carbon dioxide will decrease.

'Despite the current increase in global carbon dioxide levels caused by increased human energy consumption and especially the burning of fossil fuels, the longer-term global trend is for a decrease.

'At the dawn of life, the carbon dioxide concentration was 20 times higher than now, and it has been falling steadily over the intervening 3,500 million years. This steady fall in carbon dioxide, a greenhouse gas, acts as a buffering system, maintaining the Earth's temperature near its present level. This it will continue to do until there is almost no carbon dioxide in the environment, when the Earth's temperature will start to rise.

'Carbon dioxide is a vital part of our atmosphere as it provides the carbon source for all photosynthetic plants which can absorb carbon dioxide by using light energy from the Sun. The minimum level of carbon dioxide at which photosynthesis can occur in most plants is 0.015 per cent of the total atmosphere.

'This critical level, Lovelock calculated, will be reached in 100 million years' time. With plants unable to survive, the whole animal kingdom would starve. Life as we know it would end. Calderia and Hastings recalculated Lovelock's prediction using a more detailed computer model, and predicted that the biosphere will be able to survive for another 1,000 million years. They made several assumptions in their model, one of which was that volcanic carbon dioxide emissions would remain constant (some research suggests they may increase) and so ignored any effect that increased cloud-cover will have in slowing warming by sunlight reflection.

'They also allowed for the fact that some plants, particularly those living in arid climates, are able to use carbon dioxide more efficiently and can photosynthesise until carbon dioxide reaches around 0.001 per cent. Temperature regulation by carbon dioxide will last only 900 million years, before the Earth starts to warm, though a biosphere dominated by these plants could last for perhaps 1,500 million years at the most.

'After that it really will be the beginning of the end. The average global temperature will exceed 50 degrees C, a temperature above which little can survive. The atmosphere will become more and more humid, which will in turn enhance warming, because water vapour is a powerful greenhouse gas. As the temperature rises beyond 80 degrees C and the Sun continues to grow brighter, water will start to split into its component parts, hydrogen and oxygen, and the hydrogen will be lost to space.

'The eventual total loss of surface water will halt the weathering of silicate rocks, and a build-up of volcanic carbon dioxide will occur. A lifeless climate similar to that of Venus will prevail on Earth.

'This may be the fate awaiting our planet, but who can say whether human beings will be around to witness it? Collision with a large asteroid, or our own environmental destructive recklessness, may spell a quicker end.'

And that is the scientific outlook in a nutshell. From what Danuih has told us, however, it seems that humankind will have long since departed prior to the final days as outlined or, as Danuih would doubtless prefer to say, her body will rest sterile in her old age, her old bones gently warmed by her parent star, until the time comes for her to vacate. Then her body that was will be drawn back into the bosom of her mother, the Sun.

THE VIRUS AND HUMAN DISEASES

Regarding the virus, I am being besieged by people asking me whether AIDS is part of it. From what Danuih has said I rather gather that although its effects are far too broad to be pinned on any one particular manifestation of chaos, accelerated degeneration of the immune system will constitute a prime factor in loss of life over the lead-up period. We should also keep our eyes open for those diseases associated with the inflexibility imposed by an over-emphasis of order. As a healer of many years' experience I could not help observing how certain personality types were more prone to one kind of ailment than another. For example, excessive rigidity of thought and action tended to give rise to the kind of illnesses that restrict physical movement, while chaos in a system is easily identifiable in such afflictions as cancer.

The fact is, however, that the virus is affecting us all in one way or another. Even if we are escaping physically, the mental pain we endure as a result of our personal rejection of the amoral standards now imposed upon us by today's society on the one hand, or simply by being aware of the suffering of others on the other, can be excruciating.

I must say I thoroughly agree with Danuih regarding the way many people who see themselves as 'enlightened' worship at the shrines of anything purporting to communicate from supraphysical sources. Someone recently tried to sell me a type of military uniform which, they assured me, would guarantee me a seat on a special UFO from which one could view the pole shift from a safe distance. The irony of it was the more expensive and fancy the uniform, the better the seat! *and they actually believed it!*

As to Danuih's remark concerning the treatment of animals as lesser beings by those religions which claim they have no souls and therefore do not matter, it might pay one to see what the Founders had to say on this point although, sadly, such truths, if they ever existed, have obviously been well and truly removed by now, so judgment needs to be reserved.

HUMAN GENDER ERRORS

I have already discussed the gender problem at some length with my Crystal and Paschat friends (see *The Paschats and the Crystal People*) and although Danuih did not raise the point of a female v. a male deity, from her reference to an 'infinite number of cells' one can only draw the conclusion that such a multifaceted organism would obviously embrace both male/female, anima/animus, positive/negative, yin/yang, active/passive, or any other title you may care to assign to the principles involved. As to the viral effect on males, scientists now tell us that a rogue gene is setting off aggression in men, the inference being that some men are 'born bad'.

An article in *The Daily Mail* (22nd October 1993), by medical correspondent Jenny Hope (no relation that I know of!), refers to the defective gene as causing a build-up of natural chemical messengers in the brain 'which leads to an overreaction to provocation'. Hope tells us:

'Women's behaviour is not affected, according to Dutch research. But they must be carriers and pass the gene on to their sons.

'The genetic defect has been identified so far in only one extended family according to the report in Science magazine. However, the research could have wider implications by paving the way for the discovery of similar genetic mutations that might contribute generally to aggressive behaviour.

'The family on which the research focussed has a history of violent and abnormal behaviour stretching back several generations.

'Altogether 14 men were affected and their bad behaviour ranged from impulsive aggression and arson to attempted rape and exhibitionism. They also had learning difficulties.

'Dr. Han Brunner, who led the research team at the University Hospital, Nijmegen, narrowed down the search to a stretch of genetic material responsible for producing an enzyme that prevents a build-up in the brain of chemicals which trigger nerve impulses.

'Research showed a lack of the enzyme Monoamine Oxidase A, which allows a build-up of brain chemicals that results in over-activity under stress.

'The link between the enzyme shortage and abnormal aggressive behaviour needs further investigation, say the researchers.

'The possibility of dietary "triggers" for aggressive behaviour, which act by temporarily creating an enzyme deficiency, also needs to be explored, said Dr. Brunner.

'Steve Jones, professor of genetics at University College, London, said the biological mechanism put forward by the research was a sensible one. "But it doesn't mean they have found the gene for aggression," he said. "They may have discovered a genetic mechanism that predisposes to aggression, but the cause of aggression is not as simple as one genetic defect. It could involve the movement of the threshold for aggressive behaviour in some people."'

Interesting, no? And that came through my door, along with a bundle of other useful clippings carefully collected for me by a good friend, *after* Danuih had stated her piece!

As for the hormonal effect on women mentioned by Danuih, this is not the first time I have encountered this idea in metaphysical teachings. We all know that the Moon affects not only the female menses but also other phases in the cycle of female life as I can personally vouch for. But were we women blessed with less frequent periods we would all heave a great sigh of relief and the population explosion would probably cease forthwith. Perhaps this is exactly what Danuih has in mind, bless her!

However, logic dismisses this concept as over simplistic since anthropological research affirms that it was around the time of 'Lucy' (3.3 million years ago or thereabouts - see Chapter 2) that our forebears ceased to go on heat like other mammals. As there seems to be little, if any, evidence as to the length of those earlier fertility cycles, room is left for further research and debate. Perhaps there are other factors involved in the frequency of the feminine menses which could be, for example, related to astrological aspects in the individual birth chart. We will just have to wait and see.

Danuih's comment regarding the female brain remaining active longer naturally begged investigation. From what I was able to ascertain it seems that men's brains deteriorate three times faster than those of women. A study carried out at Pennsylvania University by Dr. Ruben Gur of the human behaviour laboratory showed that men's brain cells die off more rapidly than women's, the first to die off being those responsible for reasoning! Dr. Gur believes his finding explains why old men are usually far grumpier than old women, although he also suggests that his discoveries should lead to a reversal of the present retirement ages where women retire earlier than men! Well, well!

SIRIUS AND TIME

Regarding Danuih's Egypt/Sirius comments: in a book published early in 1994 the author claimed to have made the great discovery that the ancient Egyptians worshipped Sirius and Orion, which conclusion he arrived at after studying alignments between certain chambers in the great pyramid and said stars. The work received a great deal of publicity and was even deemed worthy of a special television programme. One wonders what reading matter these researchers worked from since this knowledge has been in existence in both Egyptological and metaphysical circles for centuries. My own book, *Ancient Egypt: The Sirius Connection*, for example, covers the subject in some detail as well as displaying the relative illustration on its front and back covers. My commentary, however, was not accompanied by the kind of mathematical correlation beloved of sacred geometry buffs: perhaps it was that or, maybe, I just didn't attend the right university!

On the subject of Time I can add little, if anything, since I have covered it from many angles in *Time: The Ultimate Energy*. However, since this was published in 1991 I have gathered lots more material, much of which involves the kind of technical data Stephen Hawking felt was best omitted from any publication aimed to catch on with the general public. Since my sources lie mainly in the somewhat questionable realms of as yet unproven theoretical physics (and metaphysics, for that matter), perhaps the least said at this point the better.

DANUIH'S CANCERIAN RULERSHIP

What did greatly intrigue me was Danuih's pronouncement that she, and not her satellite, was the rightful ruler of the zodiacal sign of Cancer. It all makes such good astrological sense when you think about it; she is, after all, a water planet and, although astronomers recently claim to have discovered ice on the Moon, one cannot compare this with the great, living oceans that cover most of Danuih's body. Strangely enough I had a dream some thirty or more years ago which I did not understand at the time but it stayed so firmly etched in my mind that I have often repeated it to my students. I would like to share it with my readers as it confirms what Danuih has just told me while also explaining its enigmatical content.

THE DREAM:
  The scenario was a wide, primitive, deserted coastline. The sky was a different colour from what we now see as we peer aloft but I cannot clearly recall how or why. I seemed to be hovering above, the sea being to my right and some cliffs to my left. On this bleak land-side an enormous crab was standing looking seawards. I followed its gaze and observed people emerging from the watery depths, young people, full of energy and bursting with questions. The first ones to arrive seated themselves in rows along the rough beach as if they knew that the crab was about to speak. Now I knew that the crab was a female, and yet when it did speak the voice was that of a cultured man - anima/animus, no doubt. The young people, who seemed to be fired with an enthusiasm for life and an insatiable curiosity, started to put their questions to the crab .

  ' "Tell us about this planet, have you been here long?"
  'The crab answered: "Yes, long before your species made an appearance."

  'The next question was "Were you and your kind the first here or did anyone precede you?"
  'The crab replied, "Other species preceded us, but the first here were the Old Ones."
  ' "And who might the Old Ones be?"

  'The questions were coming thick and fast as wave upon wave of "new" humans came out of the waters to join their companions on the shoreline.
  ' "The Old Ones created the stars; they are all knowing and all-caring."
  ' "How wonderful, will they ever come and live among us, we would love and cherish such power and wisdom."
  ' "On the contrary, you would immediately seek to destroy them, reject such wisdom as they have to give, and denigrate them as being 'peculiar', odd and out of touch with your own group-society."
  ' "Never," the young people protested.

' "Oh yes," the crab replied, and it pointed a claw to a small cottage resting on the hill above, which seemed totally out of time-context with the rest of the scenario. It continued, "In that cottage in future years will live an old lady whom your kind will laugh at and deride, and yet she will be closer to the Old Ones than your species will ever be while they live on the surface of this, my planet." '

At which point I woke up.

A psychoanalyst's speciality and an evolutionist's delight, no doubt, guaranteed to promote an exchange of opinions on the ever thorny nature/nurture controversy. Hominids are water creatures after all, while crustaceans existed on Danuih's body long before the advent of *Homo sapiens*. We must carry much of this information in our genes if we only knew how to access it but, since entry to the relevant data banks is dependent upon field band-width, a comprehensive understanding of such matters is confined to the few, and even they have limitations which predispose them to error. In the 'nature/nurture' debate, years of experience and observation have led me to camp with the former. Blaming one's inadequacies on childhood traumas is always a good excuse, since chaos can actually be utilized to good effect if the difficult experiences are treated as lessons. After all, the skilful negotiation of the chaos/order cycle surely constitutes life's *raison d'être*. Succumbing to its wiles can only serve to land us with yet another round or so in this, or perhaps some other far more trying physical world.

ASTROLOGY AND THE FIELD THEORY

While on the subject of astrology, astrologers themselves are not the only ones to have observed the obvious field interaction between planetary bodies and all other life forms. Both those early civilizations whose religion was structured around a belief in the influence of external energy-fields and the primitive tribes with which they coexisted, realized fully the effects of stellar and other celestial phenomena on the human and animal soma and all other life forms on Earth. In recent years and, lacking the backing of another Newton, astrology has become one of the whipping-boys most favoured by the scientific establishment. Of late, however, the work of Professors Roberts and Bohm and biologist Dr.Rupert Sheldrake have served to shed light on the authenticity of the astrological premise.

Peter Roberts, former head of Systems Analysis Research Unit in the Department of the Environment and Professor in the Department of Systems Science in London City University, presented a valuable case for interpreting astrology in a wider context in his book, *The Message of Astrology. The new vitalism and what it means for our Future* (Aquarian Press, 1990). Roberts ascribes a new frame of reference to astrology which he views in the vitalism context, the 'new' prefix being added to distinguish it from the vitalism of antiquity. Roberts extends the application of vitalism from the realm of biology to introduce the concept of a 'planning entity' that pre-exists before birth (and conception) and survives after death. Roberts sees this 'planning entity' (the field or psyche), being equipped with some kind of receptor organ or organs attuned to the cosmic influences of the planets, as offering a key to the deeper understanding of astrology. This suggests (as metaphysicists are well aware of, and I have already covered in earlier chapters) that the ensouling field enters its body with an albeit subconsciously pre-programmed blueprint, to be triggered off at each phase of existence by the influences from planetary fields. Roberts' sources include Sheldrake's work on morphogenetic fields and the inevitable Gauquelin statistics.

This information certainly begs comment from Danuih and, with so many other questions still unanswered and only two more chapters to go, we need as much help and advice as she is prepared to give, so I think the time has come for me to hand over to her once again.

Chapter 11

MORE PLEASE, DANUIH

ON PROPHECY

D: I observe the number of points you still wish to raise with me, so I am taking your proverbial bull by the horns and plunging straight into the next question (which I perceive you have in our mind). The legion of prophecies that are tumbling forth from all directions at present - are any of them accurate and, if so, which ones? I suppose you will expect me to commence with Nostradamus about which I have little to say other than that many of his versicles were prompted by rational deduction rather than time-probing, in much the same way that your scientists and statisticians make their long-term forecasts for the economy. This does not mean, however, that he was completely without fore-sight, and the same goes for other earlier icons of prophecy such as Mother Shipton, the Brahan Seer, and the numerous canonized personalities from within the confines of the major religions, as many were indeed gifted. But where they fell down as prophets of the future was in their insistence upon translating everything they sensed or saw in terms of the current religious, nationalistic or political scenarios extant in their time.

The true seer overrides such contingencies, which is why he or she is seldom acknowledged, let alone listened to. There is a wealth of literature flooding your markets at the moment, much of which outlines the old prophecies in considerable detail. So, if you doubt my words, why not read it up and make your judgments as each event occurs or fails to so do as the case may be.

In more recent times the list is undoubtedly headed by Edgar Cayce who certainly accessed the collective unconscious although he, too, was unable to cast aside his earlier religious programming sufficiently to allow a clearer channel for a detached and more secular approach.

In viewing some of the highly suspect literature via the brain of my field to field contact with Murry, my advice to all would be to treat much of it with a pinch of salt, especially when it comes to the details since I and my kind have not as yet decided those, anyway. Only the Time Lords are fully cognizant of the end results which, little by little, they release to their progeny. Which is bound to give rise to the question as to how these 'Time apprentices' may be recognized?

First I must tell you that they are few and far between, but I am happy to give my readers a few guidelines. Watch for the seer or mystic who has no affiliations to any existing belief, creed, or political structure; who is not interested in material gain of any kind, who carefully avoids the roles of both leader and follower and who waits patiently and longingly for their own demise when they know they will return whence they came, their task as far as I am concerned being completed. Such people will be ultra-sensitive and usually have difficulty coping with the everyday things of life. They will acknowledge the life force in everything from the smallest particle to the greatest conceivable mass, and they will eschew fame, fortune and that odious thing referred to as 'the publicity machine'. In other words, they will be difficult to find and even more difficult to pin down and, on top of all that, the likelihood is that they will deny absolutely being anything special. That is all I wish to say on the subject.

On the more rational side, however, it might pay those interested to read the experiments in hypnotic progression (as opposed to regression) and I shall ask Murry to tell you about her own interview with the well known psychiatrist Dr. Charlotte Wolfe.

M: That interview happened years ago when I was in my twenties. Dr. Wolfe invited me to tea one day having heard about my dreams of a pole shift. I recall asking her if I was going nutty. She reassured me that this was not the case; I was simply one of many who had undergone similar experiences. She explained that, in fact, only two days prior to my visit she had been consulted by a gentleman in high governmental office who had been plagued by a similar dream to my own, even down to the details. Coming events, it seems, inevitably cast their shadows and the fixing of the photographic print would seem to be the designated all-clear for its release to the collective unconscious of the species or genus concerned as the case may be. May I therefore ask you, Danuih, has your pole shift reached that stage in the printing process?

THE FINAL STAGE?

D: It has indeed although, once my external contact has been effected, there will be final details which are entirely up to me. Incidentally, may I suggest that those interested in these future events trust their own 'gut' feelings rather than some of the rubbish that is put forth as 'prophetic'. After all, what I hear referred to as the 'ordinary people' are often nearer to me than the overtly left brain logicians, or irrational over-accentuated right-brain ranters. The 'person in the street' will inevitably get the feeling that something is radically wrong; in fact, many have already!

THE POST-TILT WORLD

M: Danuih, can you please give us any idea of the kind of world that will follow your tilt, possible changes in weather patterns, for example, which countries will be adversely or conversely affected; how long the dust will take to settle and what percentage of today's population will be left?

D: The weather patterns on my surface will certainly change drastically and it will take all of three years for the 'dust' to settle, as you put it. As to the percentage of population that will survive (I am having to probe Murry's mind here for a suitable parallel) shall we say about a quarter? You see, some of the lands that will either vanish beneath the oceans or become icebound at what will be the future North and South Poles are among the most highly populated at present. I did warn my readers earlier that I would be effecting an extremely radical cull! Where there is now cold and ice there will be heat and where there is now heat there will be varying degrees of cold ranging from the kind of temperatures at present experienced in northern Europe to polar conditions. The moderate climates of your present era will give way to the semi-tropical and vice versa.

There will be a cold period immediately following the final phase of my axis tilt owing to the Sun being temporarily obscurred by dust and vapour. Once this has cleared survivors will view that orb from a different angle, while a degree of high vapour mist will give it a slightly different appearance from what is now seen. Sea levels will be much lower than they are today and tides will not operate in the same way that they do at present; which should give my readers another clue as to what is likely to take place at the interplanetary level. Those scientists who are predisposed to this picture of my body's future have, in fact, arrived at a more accurate assessment than ninety-nine per cent of your seers.

THE OZONE OPENING

M: Thank you, Danuih. And now I have been asked to question you regarding the opening hole in your ozone layer.

D: I am perfectly capable of opening and closing my own ozone layer and do not require help from your pollution or CFCs. In fact, I have opened and closed it myself several times prior to past pole shifts, although I have to admit that the pollution from hominid sources was not so bad then. There was, however, pollution from another source, which I seem to think some scientists have already worked out for themselves. Why do I need to open my ozone layer? Why do you open a door? To effect an entrance or exit, of course. Likewise I need to let something out and something in. Enough said.

CELESTIAL BODIES ON COLLISION COURSES

M: Our scientists have been plotting all sorts of cosmic bodies
    floating about in space, some larger pieces of which seem
    doomed to collision courses in the not too distant future. If
    I outline one or two of these could you comment as to their
    possible trajectories, also any damage likely to be effected
    either to their place of impact, be that on another planet, or
    our own Earth should that be the case?

D: I suppose it is the comet named Shoemaker-Levy the 9th
    to which you mainly refer, the shattered pieces of which
    are expected to crash into Jupiter over a period of approx-
    imately seven days commencing around 16th July, 1994 (I
    am lifting this information from your brain, sister, so I hope
    for your sake it is correct!), at a speed of 133,000 miles per
    hour, causing a lighting display of some magnitude. Unfor-
    tunately, because the intruder will land on the hidden side
    of Jupiter, the full fireworks will not be visible from my sur-
    face but, with a little luck (?) your Galileo camera may be
    able to record it. I observe that your scientific opinion in-
    clines to the idea that the climate of Jupiter will undergo a
    radical change following impact and, were there life
    thereon, all would be eradicated.
        Well, well! Here we have a classic example of a quantum
    leap to a new status that will be precipitated by the intrusion
    of an external body. In the light of what I have said previously,
    surely it should strike many of my readers that Jupiter is a
    willing party to this event, the time having arrived in his
    evolutionary cycle when, like me, he is ready to transmute his
    energies?
        And what effect will all this have on my body and the life
    forms dwelling thereon? Let us return to the pebble-in-the-
    pond analogy I gave earlier (see Chapter 9 page 119); apply
    a little scientific commonsense and, assuming one is
    sufficiently open-minded to view the situation cosmically,
    one might arrive at the conclusion that waves of energy,
    ripples, if you like, will inevitably arrive at my doorstep.
    These I shall utilize as instructed to aid my own quest. A
    timely word of advice, however; watch for the Jupiter Effect
    on the planets beyond him, notably my eccentric old relative

Uranus.

But to return to any possible effects on humankind, or any of the other life forms on and around my surface. Expect even more drastic changes in weather conditions, a further 'rattling' of your beloved 'constants', and an acceleration in the movement of that ever widening chasm that will inevitably separate your species into two distinct categories: those who support chaos and those on the side of order. And I am not referring here to civil statutes but rather to what might be viewed as 'God's Laws' but which, to me, are simply manifestations of the cosmos as it is and always will be. So, enjoy the firework display and I will enjoy my new medicine which I know can do me nothing but good.

M: Sorry, Danuih, but due to the fact that H.A. mentioned the possible involvement of Uranus way back in the fifties I simply have to ask if you can fill in some details.

D: How about you filling in a few facts to start with. After all, they may even provide the answer you seek.

M: Well, we know that its most striking feature is its colour, which is greenish blue (most of the other planets appear as greyish or brownish except Earth, which is an exquisite shade of blue). Uranus lies on its side and its winds blow in a retrograde direction, contrary to what is normal in the solar system. Voyager 2 discovered it to be covered not by gases as expected but by water. Although enshrouded by gases below these there is an immense layer - 6,000 miles thick - of superheated water with a temperature as high as 8,000 degrees Fahrenheit. The rocky core is believed to produce radioactive elements responsible for the immense heat. There are also several other anomalies which, I feel, form part and parcel of the erratic and disruptive nature attributed to this planet by astrologers.[2]

D: And is his influence not associated with the Aquarian Age, and is he also not known as The Great Awakener? From what you have described he must surely appear to even the most rationally orientated astronomers as something of an enigma, and an unstable one also! As to his role in my Rite of Passage, although his involvement has been intimated by those wiser than myself I have been denied access to the specific details.

NEW MOVEMENTS OBSERVED IN THE UNIVERSE

M: While on the subject of the cosmos, I have been requested to ask for your comments regarding the new globular cluster 47 Tucanal, believed to be seventeen billion years old, also the Sagittarius dwarf galaxy that is slowly intruding into our Milky Way galaxy?

D: Oh, so I am an astronomer now, am I! Regretfully, I do not possess an encyclopedic knowledge of galactic movements since these are orchestrated at a higher level to which I have not yet acceded. In fact, sister, you could tell them more about this as you have been there and had a look round. So why don't we leave it until the next chapter when I intend to play a little game with you.

M: Whoops - sorry! I don't think I'm looking forward too much to that, Danuih.

D: Let me put it this way; my brother Jupiter is about to receive a shake-up, so am I; so I, in turn, shall pass it on to you. Why not wait until you see what I have in mind for you, anyway. I can assure you that it does not bite!

M: Message received - smoke signal comprehended. While on the subject of the cosmos, the late Itzhak Bentov, scientist and metaphysicist, coined the phrase: 'The Universe is a machine for the distillation of consciousness' (*A Cosmic Book*, p.57). Would you agree with him?

D: Said gentleman was (and is) an advanced field (old soul) ahead of his time. My only comment would be, which universe did he have in mind? The one you and I view from our present position, no doubt. May I therefore make so bold as to effect two small adjustments to this wise statement so that it reads: 'All universes are machines for the distillation of consciousness', thus signifying infinite plurality.

MUSIC

M. I return to your earlier comment regarding music which you 'threatened' to expand upon nearer the end of this book. Are you ready yet?

D: There is music and there is noise. Music as I understand it should promote harmony, which is why I invited fields with an extended knowledge of cosmic music to visit among you. Many of these beings were, in fact, too advanced for their time which caused them both physical and mental suffering. Old souls who have not attained to their Time-consciousness inevitably suffer terribly when exposed to lower frequencies at the physical level, to the extent that they are often afflicted with grave illnesses. As some of my readers may be aware music, like medicine, can be classified into four main categories: tonic, stimulant, sedative and narcotic. Since my main function as a planetary genius is to promote healing and harmony, all 'music' must fall within one of these categories. Otherwise it is simply noise and noise is NOT good for evolving hominids, especially young ones (fieldwise, of course).

One of the symptoms of the illness which afflicts humankind is the preoccupation with and dependency on noise. So many hominids are unable to endure silence, which is the first real indicator as to their field limitation or soul-age if you prefer. Judge a person's evolutionary level by their noise threshold and you will not go far wrong. As for the hominid preoccupation with 'beat' noise (I refuse to call it music!), this primitive tendency should have been discarded thousands of years ago. Sorry, humankind, but you are all of a quantum leap behind.

M: I think I had better leave that one alone, Danuih. I'm with you, as you well know, but there are a lot of people who will not agree with either of us on this issue.

D: As if that would concern me! I have long since given up on humankind's majority viewpoint, anyway, as it is inevitably coloured by both the overblown self-image of the species as a whole and the inflated egos of the majority of individuals within it. But do not let that worry you. I have told you I will look after you, as will the Paschats, and it will ill-betide anyone who encounters our protective field. After all, you well know what has happened on previous occasions.

M: Thanks for reminding me not to use a sledgehammer to crack a nut in future.

D: No problem. I will do the 'cracking' for you!

THE FATE OF THOSE LOST DURING THE POLE SHIFT

M: Subject changed hastily! Those who have not read *The Paschats and the Crystal People* will not be familiar with what is likely to happen to the souls of the millions who will lose their lives during your physical re-arrangement. Please tell?

D: Their fields will be drawn to other worlds where they will encounter frequencies compatible with their own, although I doubt very much that they will take easily to their new environment. You see, in order to survive, they will find themselves obliged to take on all those onerous tasks they managed to avoid during their lives on my surface. In simple words, they will be faced with the painful lesson of self discipline and hard work. Our Crystal friends referred to such worlds as 'cosmic nurseries' if you recall. Most appropriate. Babies like to make a lot of noise and, lacking discernment, their destructive mechanisms know no bounds. They will emerge from their playpens one 'day', however, so do not concern yourself for them as they most certainly will not concern themselves with the fate or otherwise of their more spiritually mature brethren.

A GOLDEN AGE OR BRAVE NEW WORLD?

M: Danuih, do PLEASE cheer us up a little about the future. Surely it cannot be all doom and gloom. For example, what about the supposed 'Golden Age', or 'Aeon of Horus' as they say in metaphysical circles. And, while on that subject, you did mention earlier that you might tell us who or what will be guiding you following your tilt; there is so much speculation and it cannot all be correct.

D: Since I instigated these dialogues, sister, I had a fair idea of the sort of questions that might be asked. Things being so very bad at present, any drastic improvement in earthly conditions could be viewed as a Golden Age. However, once things settle down, give it a generation or so and the improvements will be radical. The new frequency, which will be the one appropriate to my cycle, will bring with it many advantages at all levels and much peace and happiness. Allow me to explain: because of the virus I, like humankind and all other creatures on my surface, have become behind in my development. Let us liken it to a class of students at a school, all of whom are intent upon working for their approaching examinations. One student, however, contracts a sickness which obliges her to forego her schooling for a long period, thus missing out on the tuition essential to passing the forthcoming tests. Because of this, she is obliged to stay on in the same class for another term. However, when she does come to sit her exams, that extra term will enable her to obtain marks that not only ensure her a pass in the earlier, postponed exam, but also take her into the next grade up, so she will find herself once more among the members of the class she was forced to abandon temporarily.

This is precisely what has happened to me and, as a result, I will be able to increase my frequency considerably more than I would have done had I effected a quantum leap a few centuries or so ago. And 'up' with me to the next level will also go all those fields (souls) who, having shared my suffering, have thus gained sufficient information (knowledge) to share my laurels.

Here, then, are a few 'goodies' to look forward to on Earth

in the future:

1. Life at the material level will never be one-hundred per cent perfect, but there will be a Golden Age *as compared to your present age.*

2. In support of your scriptural belief, the lion will indeed lie with the lamb, for the world-wide aggression which has formed such an integral part of the viral symptoms will slowly recede. Different species will no longer need to kill each other in order to survive and humankind will, at last, come to understand and respect the life-force in all things.

3. Which begs the question as to what there will be for hominids and the other surviving creatures to eat? Wait and see. Seedlings borne earthwards via cosmic spores will break forth into new plant life while hitherto unknown proteins will be among myriad other exciting discoveries to emerge. And, because human survivors will gradually become aware of the life force in everything, they will be able to work in harmony with the inanimate as well as the animate and thus discover that these also can respond to acknowledgement and love.

4. Scientists working in the field of biomemetics are already familiar with the concept of 'smart' polymers, materials that can be programmed to 'think' for themselves. In time such programming will be unnecessary; the contact will simply be mind to mind or, as I am doing with Murry, field to field!

5. Research will follow an entirely different line/method, the human mind rather than the machine becoming the prime tool in the search for knowledge. In the area of building, technology will give way to *feng shui.* Humankind will develop the ability to approach other dimensions quite naturally and without fear. The history of their past, for example, will be accessed by visual time probes rather than via books. .

6. Today's monetary system will eventually peter out, giving way to barter, or a general exchange of energies at many

levels.

7. Cynics reading these words will hasten to douse such con-
    cepts with the cold water of 'human nature will out'. To
    which I reply 'human nature will indeed out,' 'out' being
    the operative word. And good riddance, say I! The change
    will be a slow one, however, brought about by mutations
    in DNA that will eventually affect the brain (and therefore
    the whole mechanism of human thinking) and the nervous
    and endocrine systems, the pituitary in the latter orches-
    trating the eventual decline of the libido. In other words,
    the 'might is right' rule which has dominated society since
    the last Golden Age will slowly recede.

8. Likewise breeding habits among all creatures, including
    hominids, will also be affected by the new planetary influ-
    ences, the over-accentuated libido so beloved of today's
    sex-obsessed masses having given way to the emphasis of a
    higher chakra.
        And if you, dear reader, fall into the category of those to
    whom this future scenario seems lacking in fun, excitement,
    brutality, or whatever, then I wish you good hunting in your
    next planetary domain, where you will need all your energies
    to stay alive with little time for anything else. And I, for one,
    will be glad to see the back of you!

THE NEW PLANETARY GUIDANCE

This brings me finally to the question as to who or what will
be guiding me into this exciting new frequency. A plethora
of names from various religious and mythological
backgrounds have emerged, the most favoured being Jesus,
the Archangel Michael and the Egyptian Horus or Heru,
after whom occultists have named the incoming aeon. But
who or what is Horus? A mythological Egyptian figure, the
manifestation of the archetype of order, just as his opposite
was Set, the archetypal lord of chaos.
    So many names, so much rubbish! Although familiar with
humankind's beliefs concerning the first two, I cannot in
conscience acknowledge them in the context of future

guiding influences. As regards number three, the philosophies of the ancient Egyptians were possibly the nearest to those of the Atlanteans and, therefore, the teachings of the Time Lord. And, although the truths behind the myths became obliterated by the passage of time and humankind's propensity for deliberate error for its own convenience, many of the basic principles have held good over the ensuing centuries. I therefore cast my vote for the Horus connection.

However, it must be borne in mind that, as a polarity within myself, although I manifest in a feminine, passive way, I also have my masculine side or animus, which I intend to bring more to the fore in future times. Likewise, it will not be the Horus archetype alone with whom I will work and who will be guiding and protecting me; he will be aided by a strong feline influence that you might care to call Bast. Personally, I find the Shu-Tefnut iconography more accurate, however. Shu is usually depicted as a hominid and his twin sister as a leonid. Together they will keep my body in equilibrium, just as the old, aforementioned prophecies foretold. And thereupon I rest my case.

M: Thank you, Danuih, for those words of good cheer. In summary of your information throughout this book it would seem that the errant behaviour of humankind, if not actually precipitating your quantum leap, has tended to make matters worse. There is doubtless a point at which the overall karma of this planet intertwines with that of the hominid race as a collective or, as Godwin so succinctly puts it:

'... the horoscope of the earth, namely its cycles and ages, are fixed, but the overall tone of human thought and feeling will determine the immediate destiny of our species on it.

'That destiny, however, does not necessarily include the continuation of life as we know it. We scarcely need the illuminates telling us that we are reaching the end of the Piscean Age, the end of the Kali Yuga, and the end of Adamic humanity, to be aware that the present time is unique. Whether the "overall tone of human thought and feeling" is better or worse than in past ages, I would not like to say; but the overall tone of global life has never been worse. It is hard to imagine a more poetically just way for much-abused Earth to reassert its rights over us than to execute a sudden, or even a gradual return to its Golden Age position. That would certainly put us in our place! But such an event is past planning for. In one sense it is much too large to worry about; yet in another sense, even that would be but a twist on the spiral path that leads every creature eventually to Arcadia.'[2]

D: I love it! Wise words from a cosmically mature 'field'. Thank you, Joscelyn Godwin, for your breadth of vision and cosmic understanding.

ENDNOTES:

(1) *Publishers note:* The MS. of this book was completed several months before the Jupiter event took place.
(2) Sitchin, Z. *Genesis Revisited*, pp.10-12.
(3) Godwin, J. *Arktos*, p.227.

Chapter 12

THE BOOT GOES ON THE OTHER FOOT!

In view of Danuih's earlier remarks, I confess to being somewhat apprehensive about this chapter. Some substantiation is
certainly needed in respect of Chapter 11 and I am wondering whether I should proceed in my normal way or allow her
to handle it. I think the best thing would be to effect a link and
see what happens.

D: Thank you very much, sister. What I now propose to do is
to address my questions to you. After all, that is what you
have been doing with me over the past weeks so now I think
it is my turn.

DANUIH QUESTIONS ME

M: Go ahead (says she, with trepidation!).

D: You have asked me many questions concerning the nature
of the universe which I am unable to answer, simply because
I do not know. Now I would like *you* to tell *me* what exists
beyond the periphery of the observable 'heavens'.

M: As you well know, Danuih, I was born with the ability to
time-travel. I was also fully aware of the life/death cycle long
before my physical brain was capable of analysis.
　　During my days at boarding school my time-travels often
landed me in trouble. For example, when I was about eight
and a half we were asked to write an essay on a certain period
of British history about which we had just received instruction.

Feeling dissatisfied with the information given I decided to
time-travel to the period in question and collect a few details
which I included in my essay. To my horror I was hauled out
in front of the class by an angry Nun who enquired as to who
gave me permission to go to the senior library which was
strictly out of bounds to juniors. I protested that I had never
entered said establishment and did not even know where it
was. This only added to the Nun's anger and she condemned
me to a double thrashing, for being out of bounds *and* telling
lies about it. Following that horrendous incident I never
dared mention my time-travels in any school work I was
given, having realized that all they wanted was what had been
taught and nothing more.

In subsequent years I have also been careful not to disclose
anything I see in the past or future that might cause anguish
or suffering to those with whom I mix. It really does pay the
One Eyed Man in the City of the Blind to act dumb, the role
of heretic often heralding the stake!

MY OWN JOURNEYS THROUGH TIME

But let us return to my more recent experiences as related
to your question, Danuih. When my field moves away from
the terrestrial environment in which my soma is at present
bound, there is no time involved. All occurs simultaneously.
This is one reason why I have difficulty with such practices
as guided meditations and, likewise, with long, drawn-out
healing sessions. Sometimes these journeys take place during
lucid sleep, and at others they occur without precipitation as
did my first *recalled* experience of leaving this universe.

This is how it happened: I was lying quietly in bed,
pondering as to why the night sky lacked its own light, its
blackness being inconsistent with those visions of 'light'
spoken of by so many mystics and seers. Obviously they did
not refer to this universe, so where, or in which dimension
(if any) does this brilliance exist?

I found myself instantaneously outside the universe
which appeared as a massive sphere before me. I suddenly
realized that what I was seeing was either a giant molecule
containing countless atoms or a magnified atom complete

with visible particles. Sorry, but my technical knowledge of particle physics being sadly lacking precludes me from rendering a clearer description. I took stock of my surroundings and then I understood. When viewed from a faster frequency, this universe is nothing more than a collection of particles which appear to the observer as an aura-surrounded mass. The space between these particles is only evident when seen at close quarters and when the viewer is pulsating at an identical or complementary frequency. Further concentration on my surroundings brought the awareness that this whole phenomenon was simply part of another vast and interpenetrating universe, in which our universe was simply *a black hole*! In other words, all universes are not 'dark' and reliant only upon the light emitted from, and via an interplay with, celestial bodies.

This aura in which I found myself seemed to be a sort of 'no-man's-land', there being no evidence of life as it is known here. I therefore decided to move on again into an increased frequency. The next scenario was much easier to cope with by earthly standards in that, although I recognized the fields of consciousness existing there as being pure energy, these were able to manifest themselves in comprehensible archetypal forms. Among them I met many I 'knew'. It was like popping in on uncles, aunts, or distant relatives one has not seen for a long time.

But once again I moved on, this time into another universe of pure energy wherein there were no forms as such but simply a complete merging of many fields (souls or psyches) who felt no need of individual ego-expression. From this position I was able to see how each universe exists within another, the panorama stretching above and below me into infinity. Our present universe was nothing more than a tiny collection of particles, utterly chaotic at first glance but latterly displaying a perfect order and symmetry. My last point of call was, I realized, at the threshold of 'all-time' but with still a long way to go. I returned to my present body with a feeling of entrapment, which soon passed, however, as I effected a reconciliation between my field frequency and the body I am using at present.

As for the question you put to me earlier regarding currently observed movements in our universe, I see these as natural phenomena since nothing ever remains still. The slow movement of this galaxy towards the constellation of Virgo surely signifies a gradual change in guiding influence on the galaxy as a whole. We still have so much to learn about the nature and age of our own universe let alone others and, personally, I find the immensity of such comprehension mind-blowing. Perhaps our brains are, as yet, insufficiently developed to cope with it. Is that what you wanted to hear, Danuih?

D: Yes, indeed. The hominid brain will eventually come to terms with infinity but it will take time and a little external help. Now tell me about the 'other end'.

M: Well, that experience actually occurred in dream state. I seemed to be in an expanse of blackness. To the left of me there was what I can only describe as a kind of pipeline or narrow tunnel from which tiny thread-like substances were pouring. Some of these were in wave form, while in others the two ends were joined. I caught hold of one of the latter and formed it into a pyramid-shape by placing a 'pin' (imagined, of course) at the apex and one at each side of the two lower corners. And then a strange thing happened. Several pieces of 'string' immediately positioned themselves within this newly created shape to form a mass! I realized then that I had actually created a particle out of what scientists would refer to as 'superstring'. I also understood the process by which this superstring was continually recycled from other, extinct universes. Nothing ever ceases to be; all is continually recycled but each time at a fractionally different frequency which allows for a completely new series of experience for that or those evolving within each sequence.

D: Thank you. As you well know, I am fully familiar with the latter process since I, like you, commenced my evolutionary cycle within what your metaphysicists refer to as 'the elemental kingdoms'. And the reason why you are able to access these processes is because they are well recorded in the databanks of your field. Tell your readers about your regression experience.

M: Must I?

D: Sorry, but yes.

ELEMENTAL CONFESSIONS

M: Some years ago I visited a genuine and very competent
hypnotherapist to see if I could discover the source of a
problem I was having at the time. Being trained in the
traditional school of psychology she decided to regress me
- back to my earlier childhood and time in the womb - to see
if there was any suppressed trauma emanating from those
times. After relaxing me she instructed me to go back *as far
as I could go* to my actual birth and just before. She kept saying
to me 'go back, back, back' which I did.
    'Now where are you?' she asked.
    'I am on a vast sun.' She seemed perplexed.
    'What are you doing there?'
    'I and my kind are fusing hydrogen atoms to create heli-
um,' I replied.
    'And what do you mean by "your kind", are you not hu-
man?'
    'Good gracious no. I am a fire elemental. We are called
Salamanders by the Earth ancients. We work extremely
hard and exult in our creations; then we rest, just as the
fire in a grate flares up, only to recede to a glowing ember
until fanned by a breeze. Likewise it is with us and the solar winds.'

During my sessions with her I accessed many points in time
and many personalities, *none of which I knew to be my own.* In
other words, people believing that former incarnations can
be accessed via hypnotherapy should watch carefully for
time-travellers who are able to probe the minds, actions and
experiences of anyone they choose from the past *or the future.*
The immediate present, however, appears to be affected by
temporary blockages, usually because the field wishes to
exercise the choice perogative as a growth factor via the
experiences of the body. When this does not apply, however,
the veil is automatically dropped.

D: So you have now come out of your closet and I can openly
count you as 'one of us'. Thank goodness. I have found all
this creeping around for diplomatic purpose most irksome.
After all, it is not as if you are saying that being an elemental (and later a Paschat) makes you any better or worse than
the next person; just different, and we all know what problems being 'different' can bring among insecure hominids.

A 'FIELD' IN VIEW

D: Throughout this book you have had quite a lot to say about
'fields'. Do you not think it would be a good idea to give
people some idea as to how they might appear so that those
interested might recognize one if they saw one?

M: The first view I had of my own field was totally unexpect-
ed. It occurred while I was undergoing a session of
metamorphic technique (appropriate, I suppose, if you
come to think of it). During the relaxation process I had
some of the clearest pictures I have ever seen, there being
none of the traditional wave-fuzziness usually associated with
psychic vision. My initial impression resembled one of those
astronomical pictures one sees of the Sun's corona emitting fork-like flashes of energy. I was then able to draw back
as it were and view the phenomenon as a whole.
    The central core consisted of what I can only describe as
contra-rotating forces emitting active particles behaving
much as they do in a particle accelerator (effecting accelerated
quantum leaps and so forth). Although the band-width
appeared extensive, the brilliance of the core did not carry
to the outer edges, but rather deepened in colour and
texture progressively as it approached the periphery. A
continual movement of fractalized patterns/shapes/colours
seemed to develop towards the peripheral approach,
exhibiting tongues of energy with octopus-like tentacles
which reached out in all directions, some further than
others, as though seeking contact or communication with
similar fields. I could actually see the dendritic movements
in my brain firing their neurones as they interconnected with

the field causing what I can only describe as a continual series of minor nuclear (fission) reactions which, in turn, activated the probing fractals.

I was also aware that my field carried a certain radio-active potential which is one of the hallmarks of the elemental. This alien-type energy is something that hominids frequently either like or hate. which can prove difficult or otherwise for the carrier. As I open̄c̄d̄ my eyes I was fully aware of merging and becoming 'one' with this 'field'. During the whole of this sequence I was fully conscious and able to describe what I was seeing, in full detail, to Annette Lovell, my therapist.

I must make one thing quite clear, however. This supposed 'viewing' was nothing more or less than my brain's pictorial translation of the field energy, in accordance with the 'observer effect'. All fields may not appear like this, and the curious seeker would be advised to effect his or her own assessment which will (as in my own case) be governed purely by their cerebral programming.

MY POLE-SHIFT VISIONS

D: Having established that you are able to pop in and out of certain time-bands how about doing my work for me and telling our readers about those experiences you have had during such travels as might involve my proposed pole shift?

M: Oh dear, I thought that would come up sooner or later. But since you have been so forthcoming on your part I suppose I had better chip in with my bits, such as they are. How about the dreams for starters?

D: They will do nicely. Off you go, then.

M: The first one, which precipitated my earlier mentioned visit to Dr. Wolfe, occurred years ago when I was in my twenties. The scenario was a typical Woolworth's store *in the Midlands*. Don't ask me how I knew this to be so - I just did. I was obviously viewing the scenario from another dimension as I was easily able to walk through solid objects. All looked calm and normal enough; people were going about their shopping and at one end there was a cafeteria serving the usual kind of refreshments associated with such establishments. As my eyes strayed upwards I observed a small crack appearing in the ceiling. The crack started to widen until it reached one of those pillars which inevitably prop up large areas in shops of this size. I tried to draw what was happening to the attention of those walking near-by but they could neither see nor hear me. Suddenly there was a muffled rumble followed by a grinding sound and the ceiling started to fall in. People rushed in all directions trying to escape - it was terrible to behold. I realized there was nothing I could do so I withdrew. *I also knew that there was an ancient fault-line across the Midlands which had some-how been activated - and that was only the beginning.* Other similar dreams followed. Dr. Wolfe advised me to forget about it all for the time being, but to bear in mind that in due course it would become activated again, and then I would have cause to worry. I took her advice and the dreams temporarily ceased.

Some years passed and, as we progressed into the eighties, I received my next warning, this time in much more detail. I seemed to be on a train which was travelling across Europe from south to north. It was absolutely packed tight inside and outside in much the same way that one sees the trains in India where there are people seated on the roof, clinging to the doors, etc. These people were also laden with as much of their belongings as they could carry. I had somehow found a comfortable window seat from which I could also observe crowds of people, some on foot, some with horse-drawn carts etc. all laden with baggage, all moving north. In the seat opposite me was seated what I could only describe as a typical quiet, polite English gentleman of the old school. But somehow I failed to take much notice of him during that part of the journey, anyway.

Suddenly the train came to a halt in a station which I judged to be in northern Germany. Everyone was ordered out as the engine could no longer cope with the added weight. The platform was already crammed tight with others, also waiting for a train north, the increased crowding caused by those leaving the old train reaching crushable proportions. I thought to myself, 'Well, I am probably going

to die, anyway, so it might as well be here as anywhere else.'
So I picked my way through the seething throng to the back
of the station where I was at least able to breathe some fresh
air. Suddenly a voice spoke to me; it was that of the man who
had sat opposite me on the train. 'Please do not worry about
a train north. I am fully prepared for this contingency and
have my car here ready and waiting.' And there, parked in
the otherwise empty station car-park was a large, silver
vehicle. 'Come, take my hand; we will drive to safety.' I turned
slowly to look my saviour straight in the face, only to perceive
that it was none other than he who has taught me - from other
dimensions - since the days of Atlantis when I had the honour
to be his daughter. I awoke in a flood of tears and am still
deeply moved by the recollection of this encounter.

D: The Time-Lords' energies are so charged with cosmic love
that they have the same effect on me, too. What more can
I say!

M: Having got my act together again, Danuih, I will tell the next
dream which might give people an idea which way you are
likely to turn when you do shift your poles. On this occasion I was once again in another, more subtle dimension
looking down, as it were, on a road which I knew to be
somewhere in southern Europe. A whole army was on the
march, but not to battle. Foot soldiers were hastily jogging
along beside tanks and armoured vehicles. All had a look
of fear or terror in their eyes as they glanced nervously over
their shoulders as though in retreat from some dreadful
pursuer. I, too, looked back to see what they were fleeing
from: the sky behind them was a deep purple, as though
night were falling at an accelerated rate. Suddenly, small
slivers of ice started to descend from the sky. I have never
seen anything like this before so I have no suitable terms
of reference to describe it. It was neither sleet nor snow,
but more like thin needles of ice which increased in volume. The soldiers were obviously not equipped for such
weather as they were wearing only normal, summer-type
uniform. For a moment I closed my eyes, unable to believe
what I was seeing. When I opened them again, to my horror there was nothing but sheets of solid ice beneath which

a whole army was buried, tanks and all!

D: And what do you deduce from all that?

M: That the people were fleeing north to escape the tilt of your
    axis that precipitated the southern polar ice shifting sud-
    denly northwards. Surely it must have been a similar type
    of movement that served to encapsulate the Siberian mam-
    moths in ice for so many years? It also tells me that when
    you shift your poles those extreme northern and southern
    parts of your body that are now cold will become warm,
    and therefore habitable; unless, of course, you move even
    further from the Sun so that only those lands around the
    new equator are habitable.

D: I have no intention of plunging my whole body under ice
    or, for that matter, the greater part of it. My ensuing evo-
    lutionary quantum leaps will involve a general warming, but
    slowly, and over many centuries, until only a small belt of
    land remains that will be suitable for human and animal
    habitation. After that, farewell, fair friends!

THE DNA MUTATION FACTOR

M: Referring to your information concerning DNA mutations
    that will affect humankind, I did have another strange vision
    during my metamorphic session which might both interest
    our readers and evoke some comment from your dear self.
    I was shown a human brain as displayed in the usual type of
    anatomical model studied by medical students. Suddenly a
    small square of very bright light was implanted at a point
    about half way up on the left-hand-side towards the back (I
    could pin-point this if asked). Following its placement into
    position I observed movements indicating particle/wave
    excitation (radiation?) and I knew I was watching a hitherto
    unused area of the human brain being activated to
    accommodate the field changes you are destined shortly to
    undergo. Any comments, Danuih?

D: None whatsoever. It is just as I have told you.

MORE WARNINGS?

M: I don't know whether it merits mention or not but I witnessed yet another 'scene' during that same metamorphic session. I was watching a seismograph which was behaving quite normally to start with, after which it effected a few flourishes indicating small quakes, followed by another period of relative calm. Then, suddenly, the needle started to swing violently until it went right 'off the top'. I heard a man's voice shouting, 'What the hell's happening - my God ...' That was all.

D: When these events do eventually take place there will be none as surprised as those scientists still cosseted by their constants and all hung up on the steady-state idea. In spite of their blindness, however, I still prefer them to the lunatic fringe. At least, unlike the latter they exhibit some small degree of stability and, goodness knows, as things are at present humankind could certainly do with some of that.

M: I have been trying to work out your traffic-light analogy. Which stage, I wonder, in terms of Earth years that is, is represented by the light changing from yellow to green?

D: The change from red to yellow commenced in the early sixties, so humankind would be advised to be in readiness to slip brake and engage gear sometime over the next few years. But then you know that full well so why ask me?

M: Sorry.

D: No need to apologize. At times you are too self-effacing for your own good and need to be reminded of who and what you are. And I know what you are thinking, so don't dare voice it!

M· Danuih, will I be allowed to die before the tilt? I'd hate to be around when it happens. It will be much more comfortable to view it from afar.

D: From your dream of your rescue by your Atlantean father

you may surely deduce one of two things; either you will
be moved to a safe haven, or you will be quickly and pain-
lessly relieved of your body. Take your pick, but I think you
know the answer, anyway. Remember, Rites of Passage are
seldom comfortable events for those concerned, a fact fully recognized by all the old tribal societies who knew this
instinctively. This was why they insisted on such rites involving some kind of pain or physical inconvenience, such
suffering being viewed in the homeopathic sense of 'like
cures like'.

TEENAGE INSTABILITY

M: Coming back to our last conversation which included the
subject of music. While I am fully in agreement with you
regarding the need for harmony, are you suggesting that in
your future world the teenage phenomenon and its
accompanying cacophony of sound and rhythm will cease to
be?

D: There is a saying in some areas of hominid society: 'teenage was born in the sixties'. What then, may I ask, was it
doing prior to then? Can they not see that, as I have already
explained, it was around that time that the acceleration in
energy frequencies started to affect the human brain. The
passage from childhood to puberty is never an easy one
(but then, is any such passage?). The quickening of the physical body, when accentuated by undisciplined energies,
tends to emphasize what you would refer to as the lower
chakras and which I view as those points in the hominid
body designated for the input of cosmic energies for pro-
creative purposes. When such energies become stuck in a
groove they tend to go round and round until the mechanisms eventually wear out and thus they are unable to
proceed any further, after which disease frequently sets in.
Rest assured that in my future world there will be proper
Rites of Passage executed that will help young people to
effect the transition with the full understanding of what is
taking place. Via these Rites they will enter the Initiation

Chamber as children and emerge as adults, the necessity for a rebellious in-between period being obliterated.

THE EFFECTS OF FIXED STARS

M: The subject of astrology springs once more to my mind, while I have also wondered what effect both your shift and Jupiter's obvious readjustment will have on the Sun, and the solar system in general.

D: Are you asking me this one? I thought it was I who was doing the asking in this round. So, how about you trying for the answer?

M: Any answer I give would be based on pure logic rather than intuition, but if you insist I will certainly 'have a go'. The first thing that struck me on re-reading your piece about planetary influences as related to zodiacal signs was your comment on our use of the term 'ruler', but from this I gather that, although planets do not actually 'rule' sectors of the heavens, energies emitted from certain fixed stars within the zodiacal belt do exert specific influences on planets in our solar system. How is that for a start?

D: At last you are using that rare combination of logic and inner knowledge.

M: Taking it from there then, am I receiving the message that certain fixed stars, operating their energies via planets in our solar system, yourself and Jupiter being two examples, are also involved in future quantum jumps to be experienced in our neck of the cosmic woods?

D: Exactly, and such connections are not difficult to work out. Remember, I am primarily concerned with the sign of Cancer, and which star resides in that area? Why, Sirius, of course, at 13 degrees and 24 minutes. As for Jupiter, I suggest you look in the region of 9 degrees and 4 minutes of Sagittarius, where you will find your answer in the star system of Antares. But once again I caution you to watch

carefully for any irregularity in the movements of Uranus
and his neighbour (and anti-ray), the sombre Saturn, who
has a close association with Vega (14 degrees and 37 minutes Capricorn), traditionally the home of the Satyrs and
Centaurs?

And here is another small piece of information which
might arouse your curiosity. In addition to my earlier
mentioned relationship with my satellite, I am also very
closely linked with my sister, the planet you call Venus. Seek
the answer to this in your mythologies, for it is clearly stated
therein. Having given you plenty to think about I will leave
you with the question: When do your astrologers place my
possible shift? Surely that is something our readers would
be most interested to know.

ASTROLOGICAL PREDICTIONS

M: I have come across several astrological suggestions. In fact,
one was sent to me only recently by Robin Baylis, the son of
a dear and long standing friend. According to his calculations
he favours Friday, 5th May 2000, and has cast his chart for
12.00 GMT. At that time Leo rises, the Moon and Mars are
in Gemini; Sun, Mercury, Venus, Jupiter and Saturn are in
Taurus, Neptune and Uranus in Aquarius and Pluto stationary
retrograde in Sagittarius. It is doubtless the alignment of
Jupiter and Saturn that gives many astrologers reason for
concern.

In his book, *The Life and Death of Planet Earth*, reporter
Tom Valentine tells how, with the help of astronomer Dr.
Harvey J. Augensen of Northwestern University, he also
calculated the positions of the nine planets relative to the Sun
for May 2000. Jeffrey Goodman, writing in *The Earthquake
Generation*, tells us:

'Valentine says that in 2000 a much more important
alignment will occur. At that time the Earth will be all
by itself on one side of the sun. Heading directly away
from the Earth in a straight line on the other side of the
sun will be Mercury, Mars, Jupiter, and Saturn. Even the
moon and Pluto have a place in this alignment. "... the

2000 alignment duplicates the more complex geometric condition which Nelson found to bring the greatest radio disturbances. Nelson said that the most impressive disturbances occurred when one of the inner planets (Mercury, Venus, Earth or Mars) was aligned with the sun and with one or more slower-moving outer planets (Jupiter, Saturn, Uranus, Neptune or Pluto). In 2000 we get precisely this condition. No fewer than *three* of the inner planets (Earth, Mercury and Mars) are aligned with the sun and with *three* slower moving outer planets (Pluto, Jupiter and Saturn)." [1]

Goodman's chart gives a different ascendant from Baylis's, but as it is presented so clearly I thought it appropriate to include it.

Incidentally, this date is also favoured by certain American cult groups.

D: But how do *you* feel about it?

M: Possible upheavals, yes, but for an actual pole shift I think not. I cannot explain why; just a gut feeling on the one hand and my logic rebelling against the old end-of-century hysteria on the other. I cannot help feeling that the whole thing is going to creep up on us *when we are least expecting it*. What more can I say!

D: Sister, I am sorry that I have exposed you so blatantly in this chapter. I know it has always been your policy to keep your head down and I must say that in the climate of current opinion I do not blame you. But you know yourself that the time to emerge from your closet has now arrived, and I did warn you earlier that I would push you in this direction.

M: That's as maybe. But either way I intend to stay in my comfortable obscurity with my beloved felines. As you well know, I have systematically dodged the issue several times in the past and shall probably continue to so do until I die. There will be, and doubtless are, more worthy sybils than myself; I have no wish to be counted among their number.

This book is my gift to you, dear Danuih, and, aside from my Father, I would not have written it for anyone else.

D: Be happy now; the task is all but completed. Now you must take a rest and aim to complete your summation another day. May the Old Ones be with you.

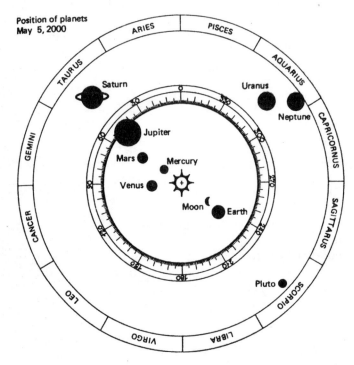

The alignment of the planets for May 5, 2000, indicating a pattern that could cause great planetary disturbances and enormous earthquakes.

Chart from page 183 of *The Earthquake Generation*.[2]

ENDNOTES:

(1) Goodman, J. *The Earthquake Generation*, pp. 183-184.
(2) *Ibid*, p. 183.

SUMMARY

In daring to present Danuih, or Gaia as she is better known to most people, in the light of the aforegoing, I realize fully that I am on course for incurring the wrath of both the 'spiritual' and scientific camps. The rosy-hued and sickly sentimental concept of Danuih favoured by many of the former will make it difficult for them to conceive either of her shadow, or her obvious disdain for humankind as a species, while the latter will instinctively relegate the Danuih I know to either the realms of schizophrenia or highly imaginative creative fiction.

However, what both she and I hope it will do is bring to people's notice the true plight of our planet and, therefore, the danger that lies ahead for all that dwell thereon. The complacency that has resulted from the comparative telluric calm of the past few thousand years has tended to lull people into a false sense of security. After all, scientists have vouched for the steady-state universe on the one hand, while the idea that Danuih's present orbital position in the solar system is fixed for the rest of her life has become ingrained into rational thinking. I sincerely hope that the aforegoing evidence will serve to shake such beliefs, if only a little, because the shock when it does come - and as sure as eggs are eggs it will - could prove all too traumatic for many. There is nothing more devastating to the human psyche than to be suddenly faced with the crumbling of the very foundations of those beliefs to which it has held so tenaciously over the centuries. As Danuih has so rightly pointed out, the tendency among most hominids is to strap hang, either on religion or scientific logic. And without that support they are left floundering in a sea of doubt and mental anguish.

So, if Danuih's and my little conversation pieces evoke either mild amusement or outright disdain, it matters not to either of us, for the time will come when those very readers will rush to find a copy of this book either to assess their chances of survival or reassure themselves (and satisfy their rationale) that the events foretold therein are nothing more than a natural sequence in the evolutionary pattern of a planet's development. Past history has shown that prophets and seers thrive during times of catastrophe; however, those among us with a message should examine our consciences to ensure that our offerings are made on a selfless basis (and not with material 'make' in mind) for, as my Teacher always taught me, the distinguishing factor between the right and left-hand paths is intention, pure and simple.

For me, personally, the Danuih experience has constituted something of a watershed in both my everyday life and my development as a cosmic being. As I write I am none too happy about the position in which I feel Danuih has placed me, but I trust this anxiety will soon pass and I will be able to settle down once more to the quiet obscurity of life with my little family of cats in a small English village that still retains vestiges of a gentle and less formidable past.

Summing up the information contained in the aforegoing is proving no easy task. Perhaps Lovelock has greased the wheels a little, but then his hypothesis has given birth to many different approaches to the Gaia phenomenon, each with its militant factions and, although I am no heavyweight, eggshell-treading has never been my strong point. I therefore deem it prudent to start by stating emphatically that if it suits anyone to view my Danuih as simply another aspect of my own psychological economy, then good luck to them. You see, in a sense she is, since both she and I are but minute particles in the infinity of creation. I firmly believe that the right of mental access to other life forms is the birthright of humankind which it has, to date, been firmly denied by the restrictive bonds of religious and scientific orthodoxy. However, if we are to judge the human potential for this gift against the hysterical rubbish that is at present being proffered under the channelling banner, much of which is totally lacking in even the modicum of left-brain logic, perhaps the imposed restrictions have been for the best.

As Danuih has inferred she, and therefore the majority of those evolving with her, are a full quantum leap behind, the inference being that much 'cramming' is needed for many of us, as well as Danuih herself, to catch up. Taken in the accepted exam context, this will mean that those unable to take on the overload will be relegated to a lower class, or another year at university as the case may be. If the standards of the school or university in question have been raised, however, students unable to cope with the new curriculum will obviously be obliged to seek tuition elsewhere. That is Danuih's planetary message in a nutshell. In speaking of those she 'wishes to retain' on her surface as against those she will be 'glad to see the back of', far from displaying personal preferences she is merely referring to the fact that those who can cram sufficiently to pass the standards required by her new curriculum will be more than welcome to stay with her. Otherwise they will go. But it will not be she who despatches them; it will be their own inability to adapt.

I recall many years ago in my youth being horrified at the scriptural teaching concerning a 'final judgement'. We children were painted a picture of some awesome, white-bearded male, seated on a massive throne, in front of which all the souls of the deceased were duly passed, to be delivered with 'heaven or hell' alternatives. The separation of the sheep from the goats was another expression used. A more logical analysis (and one that struck me when I was a child) would be that we ourselves are the judges. There is no superior intelligence waiting to weigh our hearts or condemn us to purgatory, limbo or hell for failing to fall in line with the given statutes of major religions. In many cases our choice will not even be a conscious one, but simply based on the 'like attracts like' principle. As to 'hell', well, every person creates their own.

As I mentioned earlier in this book my own father died when I was only three days old and, following his death, the family fell apart and his two children underwent much suffering, each in different ways. I was in my late twenties before I was afforded a chance to speak with him via the mediumship of Tony Neate. His words were: 'You speak of hell - my hell has been having to stand by and watch the suffering of my own children without being able to do a thing to help them.' For him there was no fire and brimstone - just pure frustration. He suffered through us and with us. Obviously I never knew the man but in those few words at least I understood him.

Prior to the fall of Atlantis, those Danuih intended to stay, being forewarned, left the Atlantean mainland for other shores, to which they carried the gene necessary for humankind's future development. The hedonists who had elected to stay with the 'good times' scornfully dismissed the prophecies of doom and destruction and continued to engage in their violence and debauchery. The masses caught in between this ever widening gap either made feeble attempts to moralize or simply turned the other way (like those travellers in the Liverpool train who looked away while a gang of youths brutally sexually assaulted some young girls). A familiar ring about it, no?

The widening chasm foretold by my Teacher in the nineteen-fifties is becoming more in evidence every day. And the tragedy is that the bulk of the 'observers', unable to decide which side to leap to, will form the mass of the casualties to come.

Since it is always good policy to practise what one preaches and, bearing in mind that both Danuih and I have effected some severe castigating of opposing views throughout this book, it behoves me to examine some possible alternative interpretations of the dreams, visions etc. that have been cited as pole-shift evidence. One distinct possibility comes to mind, particularly in relation to dream interpretation, and that is the alternative universe concept. I know my dreams often take place in another space-time continuum although I do not, however, view such experiences as alternative existences, but rather as field information probes. After all, as we are all part of the cosmic whole, it should be possible to draw from the central databanks of that whole rather than having to contribute an infinite number of lives in the individual sense. However, the possibility of Danuih herself undergoing an existence in a parallel universe which even she is unaware of cannot be dismissed out of hand. She assures me that this is not so, but then I am far from infallible so it could be faulty interpretation on my part.

Germane to this line of thought are those books relating to mythical civilizations which make exciting reading but which, when lined up with the reality of those times in which they are said to have taken place, are easily proven as fictitious. I was given just such a book about Atlantis and Mu, in which the latter was referred to as Lemuria *during the period in which it was all said to have taken place*. A little research would have informed the author as to the origin of that particular name (see earlier reference to British scientist Philip Sclater, who coined the term) and thus added a deal of credulity to her work. I am also inclined to believe that many of the strange phenomena often said to have taken place in the antediluvian world never occurred on this planet in the first place. But since I am unable to prove this either way it must, for the time being, anyway, remain in the regions of fantasy, fiction or guesswork.

At the commencement of the field-contact section of this book I was careful to emphasize how Danuih has been, and is, completely limited by my own lack of knowledge and adequate terms of reference. So perhaps it would be fair if protagonists of opposing schools of thought took this into consideration before condemning her for what could, perhaps, be errors on my part. When dealing with information external to the five senses, as any dream interpreter is aware, the subconscious mind, or right brain as the case may be, frequently communicates via symbols and puns. The same occurs between Danuih and myself; I often know what she is getting at but putting it into the language of today can prove a trial. However, a broad summary is called for; after all, there are always those readers that start at the end so it may either catapult them back to the beginning or save them the boredom of further reading!

What Danuih and I have tried to do is to render a broad view of what is likely to take place on Earth over the years that lie directly ahead, she from her angle, I from mine. Working thus, we have examined the various scientific prognostications and possibilities, and established our shared beliefs as to the nature of our own universe and the cosmos as a whole. We both readily admit that we do not know all the answers, although she is in possession of information not normally available to humankind and, likewise, I have been able to add my bit concerning both conditions here at present and current scientific views concerning the cosmos.

Regarding life and death our views concur, since we both originated in the same evolutionary stream which has helped to effect a sound contact between us. On the subject of the belief systems extant on this planet she is adamant in her condemnation, whereas my own inclination is to be more tolerant since I have to live here; for the time being, anyway. But I suppose it is a question of where and how she can be hurt and, as far as she is concerned, religion constitutes a dark area that has caused her much suffering.

The highlight of this book is, however, the question of her planned pole shift. Fact or fiction? Only time will tell. But one should beware of the 'cry-wolf' syndrome. Too many times in the past, especially on the other side of the Atlantic, cult leaders have had their followers disposing of their earthly possessions in preparation for an Armageddon that never arrived. I recall how, about a year ago, the big scare was a supposed photon belt that was all set to creep up on us surreptitiously and bring instantaneous enlightenment (to those ready for it, anyway) while also doing disastrous things to our electrical grids worldwide. Needless to say, said day passed without event while illumination continued to respond to the flick of a switch. A short telephone call to any of the major observatories could surely have served to allay many a fear.

In view of all this why should anyone believe the contents of this book? In the first instance I advise readers not to *believe* but rather to watch, wait and observe *in the light of their own personal experiences and gut-feelings*. Do not, for goodness sake, take what I or Danuih say until you have some evidence as to its authenticity. But on the other hand beware, or it may be too late.

During my years of working with the well known channeller Tony Neate we used to have a joke about striking a happy medium; forget the joke but take the advice. Taking everything science comes up with as gospel is just as stupid as giving away the family heirlooms and trekking up a sacred mountain (?) because some cult figurehead tells you. After all, as Sheldrake has so wisely pointed out, even those 'constants' so beloved of the scientific establishment are now being questioned and, from the deluge of science reports that have landed on my desk over the last few weeks alone, it would seem that astronomers, astro-physicists and theoretical physicists are themselves at variance when it comes to the nature and *raison d'être* of *our* universe, let alone its possible parallels!

On the mystical side the conflicting details, given either by a broad spectrum of entities ranging from Jesus to extra-terrestrials (or, perhaps, the religiously monitored outpourings of the subconscious minds of their mouthpieces), call for a goodly serving of left-brain analysis of existing knowledge. For although 'facts', like the aforementioned constants, can fluctuate in the light of new research, we do need a central point from which to assess both sides of any picture, while being heedful of the fact that that 'point', like the universe itself, is ever subject to change.

So, bearing all this in mind, is there or is there not going to be a pole shift sometime during the years immediately ahead? I, personally, believe there will be. My Teacher warned us of this back in the nineteen-fifties; he told us where the North and South poles would be positioned after it was all over; he even gave us a broad outline of those countries that would survive and those that would, like Atlantis, vanish beneath the waves. While many listened politely to his words they chose to ignore the content, perhaps because of its 'inconvenience' factor; to accept it might play havoc with one's personal economic situation; or maybe such knowledge proved all too embarrassing for them at the time! Thankfully the former is a syndrome from which I do not suffer and, as to the latter, well, I am now in my dotage so what have I to lose except my neck which, in writing this book, I am risking anyway. After all, everything else he told us has worked out so why not this. And as one of Danuih's 'sleepers' it is obviously something I have known within for a long time, the task of 'telling all' being something I came here to do.

As to the nature of Danuih herself as highlighted in the aforegoing dialogues, this obviously has not, and will not, meet with the approval of those sentimentally illogical people who have created a mental picture of her as a beautiful earth-mother type, all ready to tuck one in at bedtime. Her age as a planet should alone serve to dismiss this idea. The Danuih I have come to know is indeed a loving and caring entity but she is more a healer or teacher than the archetypal maternal figure conjured up by humankind. (There we are, back to the 'our image and likeness' syndrome again, oh dear!) Her energies as a planetary genius are indeed of the nature of music and healing (as I was originally taught), or harmony and balance as she prefers to call it. I became very aware of this when singing in a classical concert recently (May 1994) for the first time in three years. My confidence having been badly shaken following the break-up of my marriage I was apprehensive as to my ability to carry out the programme for which I had been booked. But she came to my aid and almost sang with me if not actually for me. It was a moving and elative experience that I shall never forget till my dying day. The Deva of Music she most certainly is and shortly when, with a little external help, she is able to effect her own healing, she will once again be in a position to fulfil her dual cosmic role.

Sometimes we are disappointed when the one or ones we love do not conform to our personal ideals. But, as we mature, we are slowly able to see in them the richness of their own special talents and, thus appreciating them for what *they* are, love them even more. Dear readers, I beg you to view Danuih in this light as I know for certain that, when you do, the benefits to be gained from the energies exchanged will add a new dimension of understanding, and therefore love, to all parties.

Do not condemn her for what she needs to do but rather be for her when she shifts her poles; share with her that Rite of Passage that is so important to both her personal development and that of all life on and around her body and she will, in turn, look after you.

FINI

BIBLIOGRAPHY

Bentov, Itzhak.

Bohm, David. *Wholeness and the Implicate Order*, Routledge & Kegan Paul, London, 1983.

Cirlot, J. E. *A Dictionary of Symbols*, Routledge & Kegan Paul, London, 1962.

Edwards, Terry. *Quantum Domains, Chaos & The Theory of Fractogenesis*, T. Edwards, Ongar,1993.

Gurwitsch, A. G. *Analysis of the Physical Sphere Manifestation, by the Theory of the Biological Field, tr. Michael Lipkind, University of Israel.*

Godwin, J. *Arktos*, Thames & Hudson, London, 1993.

Goodman, J. *The Earthquake Generation*, Turnstone Books, London, 1979.

Harman, W. W. *A Comparison of Three Approaches to the Problem of Science and Consciousness*, The International Symposium on Science and Consciousness, Uxmal, Yucatan, Mexico, 4-8 Jan., 1994.

Hawking, Stephen. *A Brief History of Time*, Bantam Press, London,1988.

Hope, Murry. *Atlantis: Myth or Reality?* Penguin Books, London, 1991.

Hope, Murry. *The Psychology of Ritual*, Element Books, Shaftesbury, 1988.

Hope, M. *Practical Atlantean Magic*, Aquarian Press, London, 1991.

Hope, Murry. *Time: The Ultimate Energy*, Element Books, Shaftesbury, 1991.

Hope, Murry. *Essential Woman*, Harper Collins, London, 1992.

Hoyle, F. *The Intelligent Universe*, Michael Joseph, London, 1983.

Jung, C. G. *The Archetypes And The Collective Unconscious*, Routledge & Kegan Paul, London, 1959.

Jung, C. G. *Dictionary of Analytical Psychology*, Ark Paperbacks, London, 1987.

Kaye, G. W. C. & Laby, K. *Table of Physical Chemical Constants,* 2nd. Ed., Longmans, London, 1959.

Lewin, Roger. *Complexity - Life on the edge of Chaos,* Phoenix, London, 1993.

Larousse Encyclopedia of Mythology, Paul Hamlyn, London, 1959.

Mead, G. R. S. *Fragments of a Faith Forgotten,* John N. Watkins, London, 1931.

Mooney, Richard. *Colony Earth,* Souvenir Press, London, 1974.

The Penguin Dictionary of Physics, Penguin Books, London, 1988.

Muck, Otto. *The Secret of Atlantis,* Collins, London, 1978.

Reader's Digest Great Illustrated Dictionary, Reader's Digest Assn., London, 1985.

Schwaller de Lubicz, R. A. *Sacred Science,* Inner Traditions International, Rochester, Vermont, 1961.

Scrutton, R. *The Other Atlantis,* Neville Spearman, Jersey, 1977.

Sheldrake, R. *Seven Experiments That Could Change the World,* Fourth Estate, Ltd., London, 1994.

Sheldrake, R. *A New Science of Life,* Blond & Briggs, London, 1981.

Roberts, P. *The Message of Astrology,* Aquarian Press, London, 1990.

Sitchin, Zecharia. *Genesis Revisited,* Avon Books, New York, 1990.

Stonier, T. *Information and the Internal Workings of the Universe,* Springe-Verlag, 1990.

Velikovsky, I. *Earth in Upheavals,* Abacuss, London, 1973.

White, J. *Pole Shift,* A.R.E.Press, Virginia Beach, 1988.

Wolf, Fred Alan. *Parallel Universes,* The Bodley Head, Ltd., London, 1988.

Some other titles of interest from THOTH PUBLICATIONS.
Available through your local bookshop, or direct from:-
THOTH PUBLICATIONS, 98 Ashby Road, Loughborough,
Leicestershire. LE11 3AF. Tel. 01509 210626.

THE LION PEOPLE,
Murry Hope.
Intercosmic Messages for the Future. The author, one of the
leading writers on the metaphysics and parapsychology of
ancient beliefs, reveals her channelled communications with the
Paschats, a race of leonine beings from another world and
another time. Covers the Nature of death, karma, and
reincarnation; Procedures of healing and self-healing; The
reality of other intelligent forms in the universe; The cosmic
connection between Sirius and the planet Earth; New and
intriguing ways of self-discovery; Why some people seem to have
an easy life while others suffer.

ISBN 1-870450-01-9 £7.95

THE PASCHATS AND THE CRYSTAL PEOPLE,
Murry Hope.
Astounding revelations from another dimension of time and
space, scientifically authenticated, covering - The impending
Pole Shift; Cosmic genetic engineering?; The Quasi-crystal
mystery; The cosmic virus that brought about the legendary
'Fall'; The role of animals on Earth; The role played by radioactivity
in evolution; Science and the occult; and much, much more ...

ISBN 1-870450-13-2 £6.95

THE PSYCHOLOGY OF RITUAL,
Murry Hope.
We all perform rituals of one kind or another during the course
of our daily lives. Ranging from the purely practical routines of
home life, etc., to the religious and magical observances which
vary according to our personal ideals and persuasions. The rites

we choose are highly revealing, as they are an unconscious statement of our real intentions and transpersonal aspirations - they are the keys to the hidden self. Contains, also, a Triple Goddess rite and an old Celtic Healing rite, two Protection rites, Enochian Angelic Invocatory rite, The Hammer rite in the Teutonic Tradition, Women's rites, Initiation rites, etc.

Murry Hope also examines the birth, growth, history and heritage of the rite, and its influence on cultural development over the centuries.

ISBN 1-870450-19-1 £10.95

COSMIC CONNECTIONS,
Murry Hope.

Following her series of dialogues with Gaia our own planetary logos and inspired by the work of astro-physicist Dr. John Gribbin, Murry Hope has reached out even further into space and time and established a 'field to field' communication on with the Controlling Intelligence behind our own Universe! Subjects covered by her information from this source to date include

There are an infinite number of universes, all functioning at different frequencies;

All universes are conscious Beings fully aware of their cosmic functions;

The role played by Time in our own Universe's present expansion and eventual contraction;

The fact that our Universe is actually a 'black hole' in the centre of an even larger universe;

The honing/refining role played by black holes;

The infinite process of birth, death, and rebirth via which the universal logoi themselves evolve through a process of continual change;

And - wait for it - the guiding Intelligence behind our particular Universe is a 'she'!

And there is lots, lots more to come!